# A BUSINESS GUIDE TO CHINA

# A Business Guide to China

15 Fallacies of Investing in China

*By Frankie Chan*

**Writers Club Press**
New York Lincoln Shanghai

# A Business Guide to China
## 15 Fallacies of Investing in China

Writers Club Press
an imprint of iUniverse, Inc.

For information address:
iUniverse, Inc.
2021 Pine Lake Road, Suite 100
Lincoln, NE 68512
www.iuniverse.com

ISBN: 0-595-26261-9

Printed in the United States of America

# Contents

# Prologue

China is a different world and there you find a world of differences.

Out there you will be faced with totally different ethnics, languages, cultures and values, mentalities, political system, and business practices and etc. etc.

When west meets east, it has been always a fascinating yet mysterious adventure full of plentiful inspirations and compelling thrills sometimes. This ancient oriental land features an appeal to the western world first as an entertaining great nation to travel on vacations for people who would opt for inspirations by new experiences for decades, and until the last 15 years or so, a new breed of visitors from the west are emerging here to look for business opportunities, to negotiate and close business deals, to work their careers up the corporate ladder. Foreigners in expensive suits are now striding around the corners of the streets in every big city, without a handy camera hanging around their necks this time. China heat was once the key focuses in the travels industry for so many years and now, it is the turn for some other industries in which serious businessmen are busying themselves eagerly with their China projects. In the past, China was already a pack of lush spectacular sceneries for foreign travelers to spend money, and now it has become a vast marketplace for foreign investors to rush in and hopefully make a fortune out of it.

Profitability is the name of the game and new business opportunity fuels the 'local motion' of a giant global corporation so it stays in the game successfully. It is the serious global players who could hold firm grips on paramount opportunities in the right time in the right place, and eventually capitalize their strategic business expansion here in China and produce some nice figures in their profit and loss account.

However, China in many ways does differentiate from the west and these distinctions lay a big gap between foreign investments and China market for the former to overcome. The gap is far much wider than the physical distance between the continents since it is usually embedded in the mentalities of the people. For a long time this mental gap separates the countries and their people continuously. However, this gap would not have been widened as it is, had there not been a combination of false knowledge, misperceptions, and misunderstanding fashioned in their conscious minds. There are yet many westerners who could merely associate China with Confucius and communism and table tennis at their top-of-mind recall and in contrast, many Chinese would reflexively link United States with fast food, Hollywood and nothing else. This naivety could also be shared by the business sector on some occasions.

Among those foreign investments who are now investing into China or getting serious about their expansion plans there, we have seen lots of those 'amateurish' foreign investors vanish in this market without a trace or get buried with problems up to their eyebrows now and then. Examples of their failures would prove that China market should not be taken lightheartedly as if it would open up to the international world and fit itself flawlessly into the well-crafted-already type of business practices or the set of business philosophies in the western world.

Believing it or not, investing in China will bring you a lot of inspiring experiences and refreshing ideas, but you also need to prepare yourself with listening ears and learning hearts to embrace the challenges. Here you need totally creative sensible ideas, distinctive practical management skills in top form, in addition to abundant pragmatic adaptive policies and procedures, seasoned with sometimes outstanding charming personal leadership, to run your business, to manage the people, to exercise practices to achieve your goals. It would happen to you very often that many business practices here in China would be contradicting to your deep-rooted mindset, long-acquired knowledge, and personal beliefs and you are required to adjust yourself to survive these challenges.

Not surprisingly, you are proud of the fact that you have survived all kind of adversities from time to time in your career life and you need not blink an eye at something that you have been so familiar with. Your surviving year after year in the battlefield of this commercial world has enriched your scope of views and made you immune to most of the surprises that might happen anywhere anytime. You also are confident in your first-rate management team to navigate the ship on your behalf. With everything under control, nothing could have slightly distracted you and your team from the corporate goals and objectives from day one.

Would that be so simple? I am afraid not.

In spite of your sophistication and experiences all over the years, business senses and professional knowledge that you would have masterfully maneuvered with in the western business world are, unfortunately not readily suitable for replication in this huge country.

In contrast to many other countries elsewhere, China forms a unique marketplace where you have to keep learning and learning since the rules of the game, fundamentals and standards applied in various industries, common business practices and consumer behavior patterns in the western world will most likely not suffice. Neither would the so-called 'best experience' transfers stand up to the challenges ahead of you. Before long you might feel an inner drive to sideline your traditional views on this country and its people, and look for alternatives. You will feel this urge, as it grows stronger and stronger along with the urgency of a need in remedial measures to safeguard your business in China, though your search will not be easy.

There are various reasons why it requires a different mindset and management approach to manage your business in China, like the barrier of language, distinction in mentality, distinguishable economic and legal system, just to name a few. In addition, there are some fallacies that are widely implanted into the minds of the senior management of many global corporations that are at the moment actively investing in China or going to expand their businesses into this territory. These fallacies would be leading many ambitious multinational corporations to blind alleys pitifully.

Yet, these conjectures have indeed nothing in the least to do with intelligence quotient of yourself or your people, and therefore are subject to one's correction if he is willing to. This saddened destiny would be reversible if they would clear up their misperceptions on investment in China, show their courage to embrace the challenges, and research relentlessly for the best business practices in China.

A correct attitude towards this biggest emerging market coupled with a willingness to learn industriously is priceless to the foreign investments. They can profit from them a very rewarding and promising future in their adventures of globalization in China, the most prominent country in Asia for the coming decades.

# Matrix management works everywhere

There are various ways to structure your organization, assign responsibilities and define accountabilities. Out of them an organization in linear structure or matrix structure are in the top list of people's preference. Their pros and cons are repetitively highlighted in many books or magazines of management science now and then and are already well acknowledged by the business sector.

Despite of the recent introduction of new theories on organizational management, which business process or customer satisfaction are asserted respectively as the core element to organizing your functional areas, matrix organizational structure appears still in the flavor of many world-class multinational corporations. As a result, many global players are having their matrix organizations across the Asian region. There is no wonder why there would be even more than one regional headquarters located in Asia Pacific regions to look after their businesses in Greater China region and other Asian markets as well. If you take a look at the regional organizational chart for one of the active global firms in Asia, it is observable that a network of reporting lines are therefore weaving all over the chart among all the organizations situated in various locations.

Apparently an organization formed in a matrix structure would allow the headquarters to keep the local operation under its eyelid and easily exert more direct control over it. A matrix structure could also facilitate the collaboration among organizations around the world, especially on occasions when transfer of best experiences and know-how is necessary. Though, these advantages could be materialized if, and only if the matrix management practices are appropriately exercised. Or otherwise, you would probably end up in a position mustering every effort to keep things marginally on track rather than pushing the organization at full force as supposed.

Regardless the lengthy list of pros and cons of matrix management, whether a matrix organizational structure would be in favor of your company is strictly subject to the circumstantial context in which you are running the business. When the circumstantial context varies, its advantages may outweigh its disadvantages and vice versa.

## Matrix management is magic

Matrix management as one of the well-known management tools is adopted by many multinational companies and was introduced to Asian countries by the very same companies from the west. In the infant stage of their business expansion in Asia, there were sound reasons why matrix management should be exercised as it has been.

Matrix Management is most commonly characterized by an exercise of double reporting line from one sub-ordinate to his two different immediate supervisors. The organizational structure comprising the senior managers therefore can be defined into two dimensions, by function or by hierarchy. The typical situation would be like this: a financial controller of the particular joint venture company in China is then supposed to report his daily duties to the managing director of the same business entity and in the meantime, is obliged to report on parallel to the financial controller at higher ranks in separate office location. The latter would probably be working either in the regional headquarters located in Hong Kong or the headquarters in United States or so. In many cases, such practice can be commonly seen on the level of senior managerial positions.

That means if you are serving general manager of a joint venture in China for a German-based company, you are obliged as specified in the scope of your job duties, to report to your boss who control your particular business unit that you belong to, and to another superior who is probably sitting in Hong Kong or Singapore, where situates the hub of the group's regional headquarters. It is imperative that you are in need of constant impetus for working closely with more than one boss along the reporting line and seeking guidance or instruction or approval on various business issues you might encounter everyday.

As described, when one of the two immediate supervisors is appointed to supervise your day-to-day work in your functional area, the other one is there for general strategic issues in your overall business. Very often, it is observable that a general manager of a German-based joint venture in China who is required to engage formally with more than simply two bosses but a 'group' of his superiors, i.e. the vice president of his specific business unit, the managing director overseeing the whole region, and the financial controller of the whole group and alike, just to name a few.

One might have a tendency to associate this with some other well-known management tools like the one introduced and implemented by Intel Corporation, i.e. 'Two in a Box'. Two managers are working together in the same capacity of a position in leading their team to deliver the jobs. Though this approach would only be viable as it was only when it is embedded with proper division of jobs and responsibilities between these two co-managers. As far as I can see in many business units of multinational corporations in Asia, There exists a main difference between these two setups: the physical locations of such two co-managers. As it is illustrated, 'two in a box' approach allows two co-managers to work under the same roof, on the contrary, matrix management would let these two superiors work in separate locations of thousand-mile-away in-between, and their communication is most likely done in form of frequent long-distance calls, pages of written reports with some infrequent business travel on top of them.

It is beyond dispute that matrix management can in many ways help the top management of a global firm to control and monitor more effectively the activities of a vast organization that consists of hundreds and thousands of staff working in hundreds of separate office locations all over the world. And it is obviously one of the well-invented effective means that can facilitate a more cohesive management system to stay in good shape in their global presence. However, it is also noticeable that the advantages of matrix management can still be outweighed by its shortfalls, as the business operation overseas is getting more and more intensive and signals a demand of higher level of autonomy. In addition, effectiveness and efficiency are always on the scale for the top management to select. When matrix management approach can assume you in a position with tighter control over the business overseas, your business is at high stake when it fails to maintain, if not gradually increase the efficiency of your local business.

## *Cultural barrier*

Personally I had been shocked at the high percentage points of the number of expatriate staff who have no experiences in eastern cultures before they are picked for the assignment over those who do. And such phenomenon seems more notable in Europe-based multinational corporations than those from United States. Many of them who are now working in China for these corporations and I would have met even have not ever traveled on vacation in any places in Asia in their lifetime before they were suddenly re-located in here.

Inexperience in Chinese cultures and unfamiliarity of China as a foreign country very likely cause a flatter-than-normal learning curse in longer-than-enough period of transitional time while the new comers are adjusting themselves in the new environment. Stress on strangeness and constraints on cultural difference inherent in an organization blended with Chinese and expatriate staff would carry in the air throughout the echelon of the organization and take long time before they would finally if they actually could, build up consensual understanding and constructive working relationships in work environment.

Worse enough, there is another cultural difference that you as a foreigner had better bear in mind when getting along with your Chinese staff. Compared with other people, Chinese people appear not used to work under more than one boss. It should have been a long tradition that Chinese is used to receive orders and follow instructions dispatched from one supervisor and, it can be said the Chinese way of work loyalty by definition. When they are talking about being loyal to an entity, it is like they are talking about a loyalty to an individual, and in their cases this individual would most likely be their respective immediate supervisor. It can be understandable if we take a closer look at the long histories of Chinese people. It may hammer serious confusion in the head of a Chinese staff if he or she is officially instructed to work for more than one superior. Confusion causes ambiguity in mind and indecision in action, both of which result in ineptitude and low productivity. Such situation might get unbearable to the entire team, depending who your Chinese staff are and under whom they are working for. A circumstance like this is always a hotbed for conflict of interests and office politics. The performance of a falling-apart organization busying itself with political struggles and internal fights could easily be foreseeable.

On condition that your Chinese staff possesses a number of qualities as a reliable staff on junior managerial level, his indecision and uncertainty may just induce ineffectiveness of the team to some minimal extent, which you would still classify as minor and acceptable. However, if he is one of your senior managers and is enticed to unprofessional conduct or irresponsible behaviors, there will be much higher probabilities that he or she will short-circuit your management system by taking advantages of the loopholes of the communication channel and arouse more unnecessary office politics than you might ever expect.

Though from the viewpoints of western modern world, China may be still a developing country and probably many people in the nation are still thinking in a Confucian's way, the fact is that they are not quite the same now. Once again taking a look at its contemporary histories, you will be amazed at that they have gone through a turbulent maelstrom for the past hundred years and been trained to be a social species. Chinese people might not, and probably are not masterful at international politics, but they are used to daily politics in their personal lives, especially those unavoidable in the workplace. In this regard, they will cope with their unique Chinese ways and in many cases; their approaches will infringe the best interests of the company, unfortunately. Office politics in a Chinese organization can just nullify any synergy effect of teamwork, if not practically amplifying the work inefficiency in the whole team.

A matrix management system very likely forces the Chinese to exercise their long lasting philosophies of survival into the working environment. Before long, their working attitudes or habits resulted from intrinsic conflicts and struggles everyday will impair the performance of the organization and dim the bright future of the entire business in the long term.

## Communication breakdown

It is not difficult to imagine how talented it requires these 2 co-mangers to be in order to keep themselves working 'closely' on most day-to-day business issues. Ironically enough, when they mistake their success in doing things hand-in-handedly, in many examples the problem doesn't exist between them, however. Instead, it is their sub-ordinates who bring up problems when they are facing mercifully the drawbacks of this system.

A triangle route formed by such three parties trying to communicate with each other on one single simple matter or a figure out of their monthly financial report would, if not handled skillfully, drag for days and weeks before everything is finally clarified and understood. The situation would be even worse if a chain of decisions are pending until an informed decision is properly made on that particular issue. The process of approaching an consensus can take ages when these parties involved are sharing little in common on their different backgrounds in education, experiences, culture and whatsoever.

If someone gets to know some contemporary histories of China and spare some time to read some books about cultures and mentalities of general Chinese people, he may find that general Chinese people in the street could be characterized by the following behavior patterns in an working environment:

- Be very likely urged by inner drive to pick and worship the leaders or the superiors for political reason or not, and are eager to endorsing figure head in the workplace;

- Be disposed to compromise themselves and follow whatever instructions whenever there are superiors present;

- Be inclined to deliver better results as good doers than as a planner or instructor;

- Be subtle and cautious, if not reluctant, when expressing their own views and opinions whenever there are superiors present on whatever occasions;

Such characteristics therefore make it understandable why on many occasions many Chinese staff find it extremely stressy dealing with a foreign supervisor of different culture because their wisdoms would also announce to them that their foreign bosses are probably expecting something different from their habitual behaviors. All these characteristics together make the situation worse when they are required to serve more than one boss at a time.

## Physical distance leads to unclear instruction

Matrix management is in favor of many global corporations in a sense that it can empower the top management to virtually have their eyes, if not hands as well, on the business operations in a remote country. What would be more fascinating than an organizational chart detailing one's span of control with countless dotted lines below his name and above half the number of all overseas operations under the group? As a result of a fact that the two co-managers and their common sub-ordinates are most likely situated physically far away from one another. When one of the co-managers is dispatching instructions to the staff under the same roof, another one is located in the headquarters trying to do the same in co-operation with the former from thousand miles away. Thanks to the technology advance nowadays, we have our scientists to innovatively build up an around-the-world giant hub of communication networks that is running 24 hours a day and by a few clicks instructions or information would be dispatched and received within seconds. Though, the technology advance is rarely putting things closer together, not the people themselves.

Chinese people are used to work closely with their supervisors so whenever possible they can receive instructions, seek guidance, pursue support and etc. Here 'work closely' means really a day-to-day working relationship, which they can meet their supervisors face-to-face every-day when necessarily, no matter how short such meeting would be. They are earnestly accustomed to this kind of relationship with their superiors in the working place. Without it, they might just run off the track due to the resultant psychological discomfort and their performance would derail eventually.

Physical distance produces very often a lack of frequent and in-depth communication to form a base on which sound business decisions are made. Subsequently it turns out one day after another that your Chinese staff starts receiving diverse instructions from both of their bosses on the same subjects. This situation would have been addressed should the staff rise up his hands immediately asking bluntly for a clarification, as most western staff would have done. However, a typical Chinese staff would keep his confusions in disguise and yet try to straighten up the issues in his own hands. He will probably not signal for external helps until the confusion inflates to a level beyond his control. A working ambience like this is no doubt like a time bomb that would be exactly the last worst scenario you might expect to happen.

## Conflict of interests hinges productivity

The most common conflict would be someone's short-term interest against someone else's long-term interest. What will you do when one of your boss asked you to hit the sales target by all means so as to boost up the total performance ratio of his region when the next one warns you not to try ever expanding the credit line of your customers or bad debt provision should be booked unconditionally? It is a dilemma of life and death, when there are only two months to go for your ambitious sales plan.

So when it is theoretically making perfect sense that both of your supervisors should reach consensus on all decisions and they play like twin brothers sending out their orders to their team of sub-ordinates, it is always a nice dream to dream about but you can never see it come true in the real business world, at least not in the world of cross-cultures.

The company would be lucky enough if its team is a team of honesty and uprightness who will not take advantages of such management chaos or the company would have to pay a high price to learn the lessons. Foreign investments cannot count on its luck of having a team of business integrity to run their businesses, nor could they rely on an impractical management system to steer the organization and the businesses as well.

## Unclear accountability is accountable

What can be worse than a situation where you cannot even make a sensible judgment on who should be appraised for a well-done job or who should take the blame when fatal mistakes are made? It would be one of the potential setbacks of matrix management that would drown the company in the waters of bureaucracy and red tapes, if accountability is not well defined.

There is no need to elaborate the histories of this nation in the past 50 years to equip you with a fact that many people of the working class in these years had been through various rough situations or just grown up observing others' struggles in their daily life in the society. Brainwashed or so called educated in the past, they once held firmly their beliefs that collective accountability on the jobs seemed common and reasonable, if not only motivating. Until now when they are awaken from the illusions of collective accountability, it has cost them decades of time to just learn exactly the absurdity of it, that impaired the national economy for so long and strangled most of the state owned enterprises to death. Ironically enough, when they are determined eagerly to exercise clear accountability and performance-oriented appraisal in their workplaces, now they are supposed again to stick to and live with collective accountability again. Surely they can effortlessly live with it everyday as they are already well trained before, it will probably be the management and the company together who are going to suffer from such inefficiency or ineffectiveness inherent in this system.

In theories of modern management science, teamwork or team spirit is always one of the core elements, which top managements of many big corporations do frequently highlight when they are promoting their corporate values. If communicated or implemented causally and inadequately, like an ill-practiced matrix management system which fails to enhance in a Chinese organization the so-called teamwork or team spirit but an official tolerance in unclear accountability, I would tend to believe that most Chinese staff can still live 'comfortably' with it, though reluctantly. Such system will gradually derail your organization into a state of bureaucracy and inefficiency where the top management will find it difficult to resume the company onto its right track.

## Divide Jobs or isolate your team?

As said above, matrix management offers you a nice idea to divide one's jobs and responsibilities into piece by piece, and distribute them to more than one person, so to speak. It sounds like an old saying 'don't put all your eggs into one basket' and it also sounds logical management risk-wise. It does in China as well, until six months later you will realize it is your team who get divided into fractions, instead of the jobs and responsibilities that have been put aside by all parties long time ago.

It must have been very ironically painful that a man in a title of general manager of the company finds out a hard but true fact that his financial controller is only listening to him with one ear instead of both. And at the same time, his co-manager, the regional chief financial controller overseeing the region, finally has shared a thought in common with him. Worse enough, the financial controller 'coincidentally' finds it unbearable to him listening to two bosses the same time with only one ear each side of his skull. Still believing that a man without a loyalty is ashamed; he considered twice in the middle between his two ears and ultimately reaches a conclusion he should devote wholeheartedly to the regional chief financial controller as they share more often the same language on the jobs, if not their own interest of career development in the company. Needless to say, the whole management team would fall apart before long, no matter which side the financial controller might have taken.

So your bright idea to form the ever most powerful management team in the company's history shatters along with their free teaming up to or against your will.

How well do you know about Chinese people's skills at faction formation? Having devoted themselves to eyewitness various political movements and social turbulences for decades, Chinese people are good at partnering and teaming up in factions, whatever you name it to the best interest of their own, or the group. And you just build a greenhouse for them to breed one faction after another, which in my opinion is definitely not necessary, if you share a similar definition of 'team', asserted by most human resources consultants as I do.

## Matrix management is a necessity?

If you are convinced that your presumed advantages of matrix management can still excel all the disadvantages hinted above, are confident in your team fitting into the system appropriately, and are determined that a system like this can line up all the components in your company to propel your infant business to a big success, a matrix management system can still be put into place for a group of Chinese managers and supporting staff.

However, precautions must have to be taken in case the pitfalls really come to life and endanger you and your team day after day. Precautious measures to take full control over all possible drawbacks as mentioned above should be always available at your arm's length and your key men's, if you deem it yet reasonable and responsible way for the top management to back up your staff.

# Low operating cost is attainable

The group's performance is measured basically by figures appearing in your accounts books. A bunch of accountants and auditors are paid handsomely to be creative when working on these figures for the best interest of the company, if not necessarily the shareholders. There is probably, if not definitely, no accounting treatment more creative than that you prepare for your infant business here in China. With such tough assignments over your shoulders, you had better check if your accounting team should be considered either understaffed or under-paid when the figures shown in your financial reports on hand are not up to your expectation.

How many times have you read some articles of various business magazines that asserts positively how righteous it has been for a fore-sighted multinational corporation to divert its investment in less developed countries and regions, or heard of speeches delivered by some well-known high-ranking executives who load tons of bar charts to show you how economical it is likely to re-locate your production elsewhere there? You can name at least 10 advantages of doing so like, get close to your market, lower the operating costs, build your own bridge-head ahead of your competition, or etc. Among them, the picture of lowering your overall operating costs in particular market would be most overwhelmingly convincing and you are tempted to follow the steps of your predecessors and start to explore this ancient eastern country.

It always sounds good, until when you will give it a second thought, then you get down to the earth, again.

You have piles of box files on the desk, feasibility study from your consultancy firm, business plans from your right-hand men, strategic papers from your team of advisors, and so forth. After rounds and rounds of meetings, most stakeholders feel comfortable with this series of decisions and your troops are now ready to fight this war in the east. You can almost smell the hopes, opportunities, and rewards that are laid in the papers of your own proposal that you and your team have spent sleepless nights to complete.

However, as it is as absurd as an Olympic medallist swimming with a lifebuoy, you do not think there is any need of a fallback plan for a good move like this. A 'plan B' which enables your troops to tackle contingencies and out-of-control situations when something are getting off-balanced and deviating from your 10-year feasibility plan is for the second grade companies only.

Worse comes to the worst, contingencies of some kind could suddenly happen in the first year of your entering into China and you were completely get caught off-guarded, instead of the third year in which case at least you might have established some footholds to facilitate your remedial measures of damage control. The only good news now is that in China you are not the first one and probably not the last one, either.

## Big is not great

It is general impression you can find much cheaper labor cost here (of course now it's a bit outdated already if you keep telling others it is China, or Thailand, or Philippine where you can find lowest labor cost and, accidentally Vietnam or Laos appear not included in your list), and that is the most sensible reason why the board of directors and shareholders would agree on such a move when senior management of the corporation makes proposals on investing in China. It is a sensible good strategic move. If not considering how much 'hidden' labor cost you might have to incur when you start up your operation and how many years such situation may remain unchanged. Then you find this business dragging on for years without high hopes that there will come a turnaround in the foreseeable future.

Here a hard fact that many foreign investments reasonably absorb lots of manpower costs by the headquarters by making use of appropriate accounting treatment to ease the burdens on the infant business would be too obvious to be reminded, if you are going to count how many expatriates are being accommodated in each joint venture company invested by foreign investments here in China. To make things simple, we may just focus on the manpower cost borne by your local operation here.

There are ways to start up your geographical expansion in this well-known growing market. In the earlier years, the most obvious shortcut was to identify a partner in the Asian regions and set up a joint-venture company in China. Surely it was intended to make good use of the knowledge and experiences possessed by such 'local' partner about the country. Nevertheless, sometimes they were just not 'local' enough to pass on invaluable experiences in steering the company to the right direction. As a result of the lessons taught after it was proven not to be the most constructive and promising strategy, people started to divert their focus and try to identify some more impressed local partner, which turns out to be Chinese state-owned enterprises. Then forming a new joint venture with big state enterprises was getting to the top of all other alternatives. Though it has not been guaranteed that the outcome would be subsequently more encouraging.

Regardless of which way you are dealing with your partner that you picked for the co-operation, you need most likely to tackle some problems at high priority before you can settle down and concentrate on your business. One of them must be how to structure and re-structure your people in the organization, in case you are partnering with a state owned enterprise. You might have seen in many cases such a new set-up may always come with a huge number of local Chinese staff, many of them are workers in the plant, and they are also the headcount who the state government makes clear to you as part of the deal for you to take over. It is the most typical way for the state to secure employment rate and ensure no laid-off of different scales. No one should be blamed for their concerns on maintaining a stable social order or otherwise. In this regard, most foreign investments are faced with not many viable alternatives and a nod with agreement in taking the people would appear the only way out of the already too long negotiation process.

Now it is vital to deploy your men into each position, senior managerial position, department head, mid-level managers, and down straight to the bottom of your workforce in the assembly lines. The importance is ascending downwards along with the positions listed in vertical dimension of the organizational chart, and the workers at the lowest level is always the least attended. It may be true that their salary scale is minimal to the overall cost accounting, and therefore a few redundancies in workforce does not at all do significant harm to the company as a whole. It is exactly the kind of thinking that many big bosses would underestimate how serious the adverse effect of your poor human resources management on Chinese workers would be and let the damage be done in the first place.

It is noticeable that state government has a tradition to protect their people with lots of labor laws and policies in favor of labor instead of their employers and I see no reason why not the government will keep this tradition in the future. After all, it is socialism in Chinese way that they are promoting.

In the eyes of many well-established multinational corporations human resources function is more or less a back-up service to support the overall operation of the company, by means of long-being-used standard procedures and policies inside the whole group around the world. Though, it would make a big difference here if you bear in mind new creative human resources function should be sought and introduced in this country.

It is commonly seen that many foreign investments handle the organization of people by a few ways, and they vary from its target group, the white-collar and blue collar respectively. They have a tendency to form kind of shadow management team composed of several own staff, mostly expatriates, to 'work with' the official management team on the list. It undoubtedly aims at protecting the best interest of the foreign investment and at the same time remain a harmonious organization jointly owned by two sides of the partnership. And for the blue-collar circle, it's not uncommon that workforce in need will be assigned to fill in the jobs and the redundancies will be kept but asked to stay home when full or partial salaries will still be collected. Are these treatments effective or not? It depends. However, you should foresee all possible outcomes before any concrete actions are to be taken since a step missed would cause you three months to fix and another three to put your team back to work normally.

To play a fair game here, you need to understand if you have the bargaining power on your investment to out-bargain the state government's desire to secure at maximum the welfares of their people. Its doesn't mean you must not agree on whatever terms set by the counterpart to take over any surplus manpower, however, you need to evaluate the whole situation and formulate a well-designed organizational structure before you are to sign the agreement of any kind.

In general, Chinese staff seems to me that they are diligent, honest, hardworking, and eager to learn, if you are capable of managing and guiding them to that direction, as usual as everywhere else. If you are not confident in the strength of your existing core management team in this area, you had better take as least local staff as possible since the adverse effect on your overall operation will multiply as the size of your organization goes bigger. Here the saying of 'small is beautiful' cannot be agreed more.

## Labor Cost does matter

When you are finished with the banquet of opening ceremony of your new joint-venture company, you will expect there are a bunch of hundreds of local employees ready to receive your instructions the next day before you get to know what to do with them. From then on this end-less story goes on. Especially for labor-intensive operation, right after you turn on the power and start up your assembly line, you will start to face the vast hidden cost incurred over human resources. Such cost might not incur in form of cash or money, but they are definitely eating up your resources and slowing down your progress in the critical periods.

First of all and it is not the worse, you are to deal with a number of retired workers attained in the deal by your local partner and the state government, and it is not simply a matter of how you are going to finance it. It is noticeable that the past 10 years state government has been striving to reform the social welfare system to keep pace with the reform of the economic system and recently social welfares have been and will still be prioritized as one of the core topics and issues by the state in their 5 years reform plan. There have come several new ordinances and policies in the process and definitely there will come more. Guess who are supposed to share the burdens of this when they are planning to make a fortune in this market? Surely it's a recognized responsibility for those who are interested in investing here. It will be haunting over you and lots of administrative costs on this mean that you are necessarily misplacing some of your valuable resources to cope with this.

In addition, not surprisingly you will need to ready your joint-venture company with sufficient funding and financial arrangements to face any sudden amendment on social welfare policies or labor laws from time to time.

As said before, many foreign investments force themselves to down-size the organizations in order to cut operating cost and improve the profit and loss picture after several years of striving for a success but to no avail. However, it is typical that Chinese employees once taken over are not easily dismissed by some means, at least not officially. It is definitely the last expected thing the government will let it happen. One trying to do such way will probably irritate lots of parties and find himself in poor position finishing the lobbying and keeping a good shape.

Therefore, the precaution to this is probably that your project team working on this acquisition or merger or whatever you name it should project a clear and true picture on human resources planning and its subsequent follow-up plan or there will be no cure to your ever-lasting headache.

## Human resources management is a routine?

Again, big organization would result in worse situation than you ever anticipate. That is why people keep saying 'good start is half success'. Unfortunately many people forget it until they are taught a lesson or several, then this long forgotten wisdom of words comes up in their mind again.

It is wise if you have prepared yourself with a relatively conservative 10 years business plan. But it would not work to the effect unless your headquarters' sound financial position can back you up with lots of funding so you are allowed to manage generously the aforesaid issues on huge amount of pension fund or compensation scheme, extra administrative costs, and to deal with the redundant staff by offering special trainings to refine the quality of your staff and so forth.

Though worse would come to the worst. Very soon you will see a generous offer in your laid-off plan would not keep your surplus manpower away from interfering your daily operation practically. I personally have seen more than enough cases that redundant workers are on strike and protest not for worse than expected laid-off compensation package but for job vacancies to be offered. When five years ago 'downsizing' or 're-engineering' on corporate restructuring was so popular in the business sector, and many people thought it as a tough job which only elite executive could have succeeded to manage it, I would say it is even tougher for someone to ploy advanced theories or methods and implement them as a specialized function called 'redundancy management' in China.

The economy of China is booming and the people here will not understand why these multinational giants with an annual turnover of hundreds and thousands of millions would on one hand squeezing in the market for some percentage of the market share and on the other hand, cut the local organization to size downwards. It sounds to them like you are investing and de-investing simultaneously in such a prosperous market.

As said before, human resources function nowadays seems a routine function area in the business world, but it is not the same in China. For those who are lucky enough to have got a high caliber human resources manager, they will understand what difference it has made to the company's smooth operation and long-term development in China. Unfortunately human resources management is never a specialized function in the eyes of many Chinese businessmen and its importance in a company's overall operation is always ignored consciously. Due to this reason, human resources management in China is far behind from being a professional field and consequently it is close to a painful experience if you are to recruit a good quality HR professional in the job market. I have never seen such phenomena elsewhere other than in China that someone of irrelevant working experiences can be offered a job as HR manager or so in a multinational corporation so easily. I personally have met lots of HR managers from various joint-venture companies and many of them were actually working in the office administration function before they switched their profession into human resources all of a sudden. Such phenomena should partially be attributed to the clumsiness of foreign investment's failure to flexibly adapt to the dynamics in their global business.

A qualified human resources manager in China should at least be proficient in understanding the deadly labor laws of China and all other related by-laws exercised by local authorities. I think not many civil law practitioners will not pop their eyes when they simply take a look at the sheer complex of labor laws and by-laws in China, and they will probably drop their jaws when they are listening to a local authority explaining how they would interpret a specific article in the laws differently from their own. A good incumbent filling the human resources managerial position along with constant attention from top management in the area would spare the company from lots of troubles that might be nitty-gritty in a sense, but would cost the company a harmonious relationship with the local authorities as well.

## Overhead cost

Investing abroad always requires you to bear additional costs at your start-up on creating and sustaining a working environment in your local establishment which is comparable to that in your domestic operation.

As far as allocation of human resources are concerned, the most frequent way is to re-locate your most experienced key managers in your headquarters or other well-established subsidiaries to the new operation in China. They are supposed to make the best use of their successful experiences and replicate as much as possible a business model of your preference in light of the characteristics of local market. And the model is expected to commence in the shortest period of time upon their arrivals. Besides, staffing in local talent market is the most crucial element in starting up a new operation as well, though I tend to believe that not many high-ranking executives of multinational giants are convinced wholeheartedly the essence of quality of local staffing, as far as what they are doing is concerned.

When you can read in countless business magazines from time to time and are aware of how often some big companies are making endless statements similar to that 'our company values the people as the most important asset to the company and etc. etc…', you should consider it merely a statement of self consolation or gimmick of public relations.

Yet your people form the backbone of the skeleton of your whole organization and how it is worked out is strictly and significantly related to how such organization will perform in the future, since these people will then take full control over setting up all the rest of the operating system on which your business relies to roll out.

So your handpicked key managers are sent to the battlefield and they are ready to fight the battle. It is a sensible move and it proves to be the most popular one in the business sectors as well, until you receive the first year-end financial report and are wondering why the overhead costs could be so incredibly high. Needless to say, you will keep wondering till you remember how much you are paying additionally in the compensation package of each of your heavyweight expatriate to keep them hardworking and loyal to you, or your company.

There are some cases in which expatriates had fought a good fight for some companies in China, but there are not many enough. When you fail to see your overhead costs go down year by year, you do realize that your profit and loss does, if you are fortunate enough that you have a black figure at the bottom of the line after few years of struggle.

Alerted by such bad news for consecutive four years, you and your fellow directors in the board would call for a mandatory cost saving programs throughout the joint-venture company. One of the measures is to retreat the expatriates and replace the openings with local managers. Though it does help lower the overhead cost on the paper significantly, it very often does not help your business to regain its balance in the figures. Why would be that? Because localization cannot always be a 'quick fix' when your human resources function has not developed a good mechanism in the system in the first place to train up capable local managers to take up the jobs all of a sudden.

Here I put the question aside whether expatriates from abroad can help your building up a healthy business or not, as I think this is also a very interesting topic we may further explore in the later chapters about expatriation of staff in your China's operation.

So the problem here is not that you would have the courage to call for a halt of keeping expensive expatriates in the organization in China, regardless of the fact that they are contributing to the company or not. It is instead a matter of whether you are, or to be exact, whether the remaining organization is ready to take up the challenges ahead with their own expertise and experiences. And whether your human resources function has established intentionally a good training scheme and schedule to train up all the potential local successors will be the next question to follow. If you find yourself unsure about the second question, then it will be rather awkward if the answer to the first one would be positive.

The absence of thought-thorough plan on well deployed comprehensive staff training and orientation programs on key positions followed by a absurd retreat of your expatriate team will put your local operation in a very poor position, a position much worse than just where you have no choice but to live with high overhead cost for the first few years and its negative impact on your financial soundness.

To sum up, if you are in a position deploying your people into your organization in China, you had better deliberate at first whether and how to deploy your key men in the new organization and in the meantime how to gear up the long-term series of training programs for the sake of staffing flexibility. Localization is an obvious process to let your business grow in a healthy fashion as long as you are equipped with fore-sightedness and attention to adequate staffing guidelines in the first place. Otherwise, such inconsideration would cost you not only constraints on further expanding your local business, but also financial burdens over your global business operation.

## Education on concept of quality

If your business in China involves production process in a plant or assembly lines, quality will be substantially a big concern in China, though it is also vital in the interest of your company as far as intangible goods and services are concerned.

Though state-owned manufacturing industries have been long-existing and Chinese seems also one of the peoples in the world who are accustomed to entrepreneurship, quality is something they keep talking about very often but seldom working on. You will not be surprised by the fact that there is much room for substantial improvement and upgrading on Chinese's competencies of production management or plant management in terms of quality control and standards. There is no wonders when seeing is believing. You visit the marketplace and you will find a world of local produced merchandises that its quality is not up to the internationally recognized standards and yet are being sold and bought everywhere everyday.

Imported international brands are then at high stake to be ruined when local production of these brands is going to take place here. The reason why imported brands are welcome and can be priced at higher end of the price range is simply because the Chinese consumers embrace an assumption that they would and should be in better quality. However, it doesn't mean that they cannot accept other substitutes in poorer quality. They would be willing to give patronage to brands with fair quality, if they are not asked to pay more than they expect.

Unfortunately there are still lots of cases which you find imported brands are struggling in the market due to its failure to keep its quality and one minor negligence or slackness in your production plant which results in few carton boxes of defective merchandise on the shelves might lead to disastrous situation and cost your something you cannot afford.

To start with quality, you may instantly try to shift your concern and focus more often on some topics of quality control and production management, including how to train up your workers to operate the machineries, how to work strictly according to well-devised workflows, how to comply with rules and procedures on the routine and so forth. It's undoubted that Chinese staff working in the plant on various levels should be presumed to be in need of certain trainings, but it is too risky for foreign investments to simply stress on technical know-how transfer, machinery operational skill training and etc. Nonetheless, when all these should be coped with, there is yet another big leap forward that you are required to take, i.e. basic mass education in the entire Chinese organization to enhance your staff's clear understanding of importance of quality. It is an overwhelming element over the transfer of technical knowledge and it requires much more effort to correct their mentality by hammering into their minds an understanding of what quality control means to the market, to the company and to themselves.

Quality control is an issue that might thwart your business from growing as you may have learned from some falling brands, which were once leading in the market. When there are numerous training or lectures offered to your staff to sharpen their working skills on supervision, computer literacy, time management, sales skills, etc. etc., I would suggest that some programs of any kind to educate and promote the concept of quality to your employees on each level and gradually change their mentality on quality perception be the top priority.

Customer satisfaction is now the most popular phrase in the business world and it is strongly related to quality of your products and services. More importantly, quality is not bound to quality of products or services themselves. A broad meaning should cover quality of works your staff are delivering everyday. Only those who believe in that quality of their works speaks for them can deliver you a good job they are asked to complete and in the long run contribute to the final success of the company.

# Chinese embrace western management skills eagerly

Revolution by industrialization and the decade-lasting on-going technology advance on computerization and high technologies do fabulously show us how human's creation and invention could help improving the well-being of our daily lives.

Every year there are constantly coming some new business theories, innovative management tools, impressive research results, advanced technology application and etc. to inspire businessmen, executives, and managers to take new height in their jobs, exploit new areas of their work, capture new opportunities of business.

They are usually welcome by the all industries of the business sector and many multinational corporations are likely rushing to introduce applicable theories and tools in their daily working life in order to advance their performance and revitalize their business. It makes perfect sense when these new inventions can make their lives easier.

When a new management tool or theory does bring in promising improvement in particular areas in your daily operation, they might not work under all circumstances. A well-established company run by a well-structured organization with a proven track record and experiences can find it easy to adapt into changes of all sort, from organizational re-engineering to computerized supply chain management, from new principles on financial treatment to computerized warehousing management. It is much easier to fit an additional module into the already operating machine and what you need is a team of taskforce to design, implement and monitor the transformation process. To them, change is a routine to continuous improvement.

However, the situation is different as far as most Chinese operations are concerned. An introduction of the same tools or measures in your Chinese operation might not necessarily guarantee you the same advantages that you would effortlessly take in your other organizations in the west. Or at least while the advantages are anticipated confidently, they are likely offset by some unfavorable consequences that would grant you no second chance to do it all over again.

## Modern management tools excel, sometimes

I think nowadays there are coming lots of new concepts, theories or applications on business management and specific functional areas everyday. Some of them will be introduced into some big corporations at large scale and there they prove themselves to our-performing those doing otherwise. Though we should bear in mind that they are applied to the 'experimental environment' on top of the existing management practices, especially some basic but ever effective management principles. I personally dare not imagine the situation where a 're-engineering' project would have survived without a basic yet viable set of corporate principles and policies to streamline various business processes; or a 'Management by Objective' approach would have effected properly at the minimal extent if communication channels among each individual department are dismantling already; or a computerized management system on ERP would have commenced when most of your operational staff are computer illiterate at that time.

I personally like to elaborate the aforesaid third example as it can easily explain how a fatal mistake could be made with a good intent coupled with no favorable environmental factors. Many big corporations are fantasized and tempted by today's applications of high technologies in their areas and sometimes they are just inclined to hustle to engulf them as they see it like a first-aid kit to improve, if not actually safeguard, their business from the edge to the cliff.

You and your senior colleague start to realize that the whole operation in china has spiraled out of control the past 6 months and you
considered all the alternative remedial measures proposed by various
parties together with more alerted messages than you might want. Now
you are stuck in this critical moment to pick your favorite measure or
measures, which should be a strong dosage of medicine to cure your
sick and weak business out there. One of the alternatives would be to
launch the powerful computer management system on the problematic
business, a system to cover the whole range of business processes, from
customers relationship management, warehousing management,
account book-keeping and financial reporting system, and sales and
distribution system and etc. You know that your headquarters and
many other European subsidiaries have been using it for more than 3
years and it have been well received with lots of promising results afterwards. Reasoned with these facts, in addition to the numerous promises the consultants from the computer system vendor have made to
you, you deliberated and are finally determined to go for this option
with an aim to achieving the following well-defined objectives:

- Build up an interface through which headquarters can monitor
  the business by first-hand figures processed in the linked system,
  other than the existing lousy communication channels the traditional way;

- Regulate the operation by applying lots of computer-recognized
  principles and rules to eliminate dysfunction and manual errors;

- Consolidate pool of sales and financial data to enable senior
  management to analyze and therefore make correct decisions
  upon it;

And here the nightmare starts.

This project goes in progress for the next 9 months and a special
monthly report keeps you abreast of the latest status of the project. The
millions alone invested by capital to this project should and need to

project a bright future to be seen. Everything goes smoothly, at least reflected from the update reports that you received from the local management. Then the first month when the computer system is put into implementation, suddenly there are alarms everywhere everyday and bad news come from all directions through your telephone line, fax machine, e-mail, and etc. to the extent you are impressed the first time at the teamwork maneuvering of your staff out there.

Everything just seems to collapse the first month. When your subordinates dare not tell you how much extra resources are needed to resume the system into working, the same consultants will be more than pleased to present you a new proposal on how they can get it fixed for you and how much.

Up to this moment everything would retract back to square one.

You ask yourselves what has been done wrong. Apparently there may be lots of areas where someone has just neglected something or mistaken some others and all of which can result in the same disaster. However, the most basic question is if it is actually a wise idea as everyone fancied when commencing a high-end management system does require the users to possess specific qualities, skills and knowledge to accommodate themselves to the new system. Sometimes there are too many top-down decisions made without a precise evaluation and review on the current situation, and therefore it results in turning a good-intended management decision into a bad joke among the competition in any minutes.

Stories of similar kind happen now and then in China in the circles of foreign investors. This example is just to show you the fact that in many times your business operation in China is just not yet ready to make a good use of the high technologies that you push on to them. Honestly speaking, it appears not their fault not to get ready, technically and/or mentally, and on the contrary; it would be a fault from the decision makers not to understand the basic differences in the environment and their own people at all before they rush into a decision by their impulse.

Chinese people are not at all against any high technologies or advanced management skills, and actually they are working hard to catch up with the rest of the world. However, in the past hundred years they were not given some good chances to keep their pace with our western world in many aspects. The only solution would be that more patience is granted and more opportunities in training and education are offered to them so the overall environment in China would be tempered with more favorable factors in favor of your local business.

The above is just an example concerning technical knowledge transfer, which I think it is already the less complex cases in our daily business life. There are a lot more concerns that are related to differences in cultural background, education, social value, social norms and all these should be considered before top management is orchestrating a big plan to muster some new management tools in your Chinese operation.

If it is not yet made clear on the importance of this piece of advice, here may be another little example to show you how it can or cannot work with some creative management tools.

In human resources management, there is one theory stipulating that a more effective appraisal system to evaluate your staff's performance is to have his immediate supervisor and the staff himself to do the evaluation together by giving scores at each criteron and category of his overall performance. When it may be kind of keep-the-door-open management to promote open-mindedness and fairness in the working environment, it is rather doubtful if it can really work to the same effect in China, considering Chinese staff is inclined to hold opposite opinions to his boss, not openly at least. A pushy replication of such tool just fails to serve its purposes unless it is planned well ahead and implemented with a good orientation program. There must be yet successful occasions in some of multinational corporations, though I am afraid that the failure rate in China is relatively much higher than those elsewhere.

All in all, if some advance management concepts and theories could be viewed as merely some fancy management gimmicks to make your company look better in your eyes, they do not look as wonderful as you would like to believe in the eyes of your Chinese staff.

## Do guidelines and regulations really rule?

Rules and regulations of every kind are the fundamentals to guide and direct your people the way they are supposed to behave in the working environment. They also define any wrongdoings by any of your staff and sort out corrective measures whenever necessary.

Unfortunately when you see it as a simple fact as just that, Chinese people do not see it your way or the western way. What rules and regulations say to them is one thing, but who set the rules and regulations is to them another thing. And the latter usually sounds much more important than the former.

If you expect to rely on a set of rules and regulations to regulate your Chinese business by throwing your Chinese team a bunch of written staff manuals, working procedures, principles on authorization, guideline on approval procedures and so on, and take for granted that the Chinese people will abide consciously by these in their daily working days, you might be well disappointed. The chance that your management system will remain in a good shape would be very slim.

It will be interesting to observe how different the result would be if you ask two different managers to dispatch to the same group of Chinese staff the same commands and instructions and review the result some time after the assignment is completed. It is not the rules or regulations itself bringing in the varying results, it is the manager who matters.

It is again an effect of some built-in cultural factors. In plain words, western people are more voluntarily and willingly to give respect to well-stipulated regulations and commonly consensual rules, and follow them closely in their workplace, whereas a set of rules and regulations written in however precise words would be as ambiguous to many Chinese people and they are likely to interpret them differently and accordingly alter their behaviors whenever necessary. As a result, the most viable way to keep Chinese staff in line with the rules and regulations is to have the right persons to convey the messages. A word spoken would be stronger than hundreds of pages in print to the majority of Chinese people.

I think 'Guangxi' is most probably the first Chinese word a foreign businessman would have learned ever from his first day doing business with Chinese. Out of such a simple word relating to 'the personal connection with other people' (here people are always meaning very important people in power), it implicitly tells how important the element of people is in the game of business conducting to the extent that rules and regulations could be slightly and brightly bent to fit 'exceptional' situations in one's favor.

It is beyond dispute that rules and regulations in form of written or whatsoever is a mandate to keep order and safety in the workplace. But they are more like officialdom for kind of formality, and it depends heavily on who is going to act as a figurehead on behalf of the company on the spot.

## Leader or manager?

There is a typical saying 'the basic difference between a leader and a manager is that a manager is to do the things right while a leader is to do the right things'.

And there is also another saying 'business is business' and therefore, in a company the senior management is always looking forward to having more and more capable managers so they are working strictly in accordance with the instructions received from the top and doing it in the right way and most importantly, in the best interest of the company. Demand on good managers outweighs that on good leaders since doing the right thing might not necessarily in the best interest of the company and there are also many circumstances under which there are conflicts. It is a business culture widespread over each corner of the borderless business world, and it is well accepted as well.

Hence, many good managers who had made tremendous contributions to their companies have been so outstanding in their professions that many of them are picked and sent to China as expatriate executives to help expanding the frontier of their markets into it.

When your expatriate team are working hard to build up your new business here in China, together with lots of local Chinese staff, you might wonder why their collective performance is not up to your expectation though you are sure they form already as the best elite team as you can find in the world.

A job here is supposed to be done by a team combined with one or two supervisors with a group of workers. They can also be defined as instructors and a group of doers, or as leaders and a group of followers. When a manager is always someone who is the core factor determining if the job can be properly done or not, many people would under-estimate what dramatic change an existence of a capable leader could contribute in the group. In some cases that a large group of people on various level of the hierarchy is involved, the manager would or would not act as a leader, but one thing for sure is that a leader could help even better accomplishing a task.

When west meets east, we conclude that western staff, no matter what level he is on, would work more independently with a modestly close relationship with his team member, whereas eastern ones rely more on mutual interaction and collective behavioral patterns throughout the process of the assignment. Chinese people are well accustomed to collective goals, collective norms and behaviors and etc. A manager with skillful leadership will make a difference in managing the Chinese people and directing them in the work to the best interest of the organization and the company. Relatively speaking, Chinese staff would be easily driven by someone who would portray his personal charisma and leadership over the team. They would prefer a leader whom they succumb to by his appeal on personal charisma rather than a manager whom they surrender to his power and authorities. Understanding it, you find that it is not beyond imagination that how a good leader would stimulate and sometimes even 'manipulate' the group members in accepting ideas and doing things and subsequently influence substantially the qualities of the jobs when done.

I think there are too many cases in which a foreign investment tends to cling too much the future of the company on few managers' performance and relies too much on their managerial skills to supervise their people in the workplace and, fatally neglect the fact that in China a good manager gifted with good leadership skill would surprisingly stimulate and motivate the majority of your Chinese staff in the work and your success could be multiplied accordingly.

Hence, when it seems appropriate for your company to initiate a series of training programs for your Chinese staff and Chinese managers, leadership skills should be one of the themes in the series. In addition, if your expatriate managers are willing to spare their leisure time for learning mandarin for the sake of better oral communication with his sub-ordinates, some more tips on leadership skills would probably do good to his career as well as the company too.

## Communication by meeting

In a lot of multinational corporations there are hundreds of internal meetings, inter-departmental meetings and other conferences going on everyday. Most of them are held for good reason. But only a few meetings are with good reasons enough to rationalize the frequency and duration of themselves.

I always have an impression that the productivity per head in western business world must be higher, if not just slightly, than that in China and therefore they can afford numerous working hours to be spent on lengthy meetings for briefing on project, discussions on details, brainstorming on new packaging, exchange of ideas, presentation of new products and etc., not to mention the time spent on preparing the truckloads of diagrams, charts, slides and photocopies beforehand. It does no harm to the company once they do not have better things to do at that moment. Surely, it does some good to the organization and the jobs if and only if the attendants are really communicating for the sake of better understanding and trying to reach agreements on the subjects on hand.

However, the 'meeting culture' here in China appears to diverge from the west and many meetings are called for to serve any purposes but assembling on purpose a group of people together in a place for discussions, exchange of ideas and the like. It can be said that Chinese people are getting used to meetings and conferences of various kind in their daily life for years. In the morning a Chinese would watch in the television some national leaders appear on the podium in a hall putting their fists in the air reciting their political views to thousands of audience who are applauding enthusiastically all along, but he cannot wait till it finishes because he is supposed to sit in a work meeting this morning to represent his boss since his boss will busy himself with another business review meeting or so. In the evening, he will attend a meeting organized by the district committee of environment to discuss about the issue of noise pollution caused by a construction site next block to your place. So to speak, Chinese people are a social species and meeting is part of their lives that you can never separate from.

However, it is also notable that many Chinese are present in a meeting to listen halfheartedly, if not absent-mindedly, as if their sole responsibility is to show up and have their mouths zipped, with an exception of those who are in power to take their time and keep the other stay as long as they like. The communication in a meeting of Chinese way is usually one-way between both parties, one speaks and the others listen or at least pretend to.

In the western business world, meeting would be the core business activities out of all that are needed everyday for one to close a business deal with his customer, to reach an agreement with his business allies, to discuss the details with his subordinates, to exchange information with his peers, and so forth. Many big successes in the history have been originated from a meeting somewhere sometime. In general, a successful meeting can serve the purpose of getting all related parties in the company together and play their parts. A successful and constructive meeting always work wonders when it offers people time and place to have face-to-face communication, share data and information, exchange ideas and opinions, make reasonable compromises and reach group consensus, and formulate action plan and assign it to accountable parties.

Two basic points should be made clear here. Firstly, one should not presume that a group of people from the same backgrounds of ethnic, language, profession, education, values, or culture would then guarantee you an efficient and constructive meeting to take place because whether it is or not depends on the purposes and the topics for which such meeting is called. And secondly, an effective meeting would be inefficient one and vice versa. Bearing these in mind, I would like to try comparing my personal experiences in meetings in which mostly participants are foreigners with those in which mainly Chinese managers are involved, and conclude my observations in general.

To foreign managers, they tend to take meeting as an occasion that is a place for them to discuss and exchange ideas, a chance to clarify and understand the situation, a channel to share information, a workshop to lay down problems and work out specific solutions, a command room to send off or receive orders and instruction. On the contrary, Chinese managers are likely to see that meeting is mainly a place to either issue orders to sub-ordinates or collect instructions from their own superiors, a channel to collect information instead of feeding information to someone else, an occasion to appraise or punish someone publicly and a stage for superiors to exercise their power and authority. Chinese is more inclined to subtlety of informal and frequent personal meeting with their superiors than many foreign managers would be. They sit in the meeting and stand by for a more or less one-way information inflow. When asked about their own thoughts on specific issues or topics, they could react so cautiously that very likely they give you some ambiguous or model answers if ever possible. Straightforwardness and openness are not their style too as far as problem or accountability is concerned and discussed in the meeting. With all these you either find a meeting with your Chinese managers too boring and silent or you start to wonder if your business is going so smoothly you actually need not interfere it with such a meeting.

Chinese managers are accustomed to irregular, informal, and frequent personal meetings and gathering with their colleague, sub-ordinates and superiors where they can relax easily but talk serious talk. On these occasions they will open up themselves and express their thoughts and comment on his work, his team and whatever may help you understand their thinking, just like your foreign managers in the meeting.

There does exist a big difference between a meeting in Chinese way and a usual business meeting in the west. The efficiency, effectiveness or productivity of a meeting with Chinese people would be much lower than the ones without. If one can imagine how terrible if most people in your company in China are busying themselves with fruitless meetings day by day without committing themselves into making the meeting a successful one. And all these unproductive meetings are actually consuming their precious working hours that would have been spent on productive works otherwise, it can also explain why such company would have been zigzagging its way to regain its composure but to no avail.

It is therefore the responsibility of the top management, who is supposed to replicate only selectively their successful management expertise into its Chinese business and at the same time adapt their management tools in the daily operation. Formal meeting is not the way to ensure a smooth communication throughout the organization in China, and your attention to cater for your Chinese staff's needs requires also your willingness to promote a more 'humane' management system, to empower the organization with managers with good leadership, to secure close and sincere working relationship among each working parties and so on.

## Trainer is never a coach

Since China started to tiptoe ahead with its determination to open up to the western world in 80's, there have been dramatic changes across the nation and one of the primary reforms has been occurring in the business sector.

Now you see the prosperous market driven economy across the territory, booming private entrepreneurship in numerous towns and counties, hundred millions of daily transactions in stock market in Shanghai and Shenzhen, thousands of imported branded merchandises on shelves, fast food chain of McDonald's or Kentucky scattering in big cities, and so on. You have more confidence in this market than ever before, especially when you discover so many local well-educated talents are available for you to choose from. They are definitely backing up your establishment of a strong team that would be comparable to any other organization you are having elsewhere in the west, and you can have it at a much lower labor cost.

It is true that Chinese people are changing their basic attitudes toward their work. They now are more ambitious in their careers, driven to succeed in their capacities, eager to learn in new working environments, and anxious to grasp opportunities arising. These potentials inherent in your local employees encourage you to blueprint a series of training programs in your establishment in China, and harbor a high hope that your young Chinese managers would further enhance and upgrade their competences and skills so that your company can be benefited in return. It is the basic philosophy behind your investing in your people.

Such thinking has generated countless business opportunities to consulting companies and human resources specialists who are more than delighted to provide you with professional advices and recommendations. There are also many global corporations that are operating their own division of in-housing trainers already and would extend easily into their establishments in China. Therefore, you have all the sound reasons why not making the best use out of it by sending some trainers across the continents to organize some periodic trainings in this regard.

No matter whether it is out-sourcing of training capacity or diverting of in-house training resources, the approach is common: get someone to organize good-titled periodical group trainings in form of lectures or similar for those with potential on a regular basis. The target of these trainings can range from learning computer software and applications to advanced sales skills, team spirit building to time management, whatever it is, the design of the program looks great on the paper and it already seems justifying the cost incurred. You would envision that significant upgrading on the qualities and competences by training will very soon strengthen your company's competitiveness in the market as your elite team polished with latest skills and knowledge will fight a decent fight for you in the battlefield.

This visionary keep growing until one year after you are told in the business review meeting that the scale of such training should be cut down to size since its attractiveness seems deteriorating among the staff and department heads and, its effectiveness yet is seriously in doubt. You cannot help wondering what has happened to the costs in millions you spent on staff training and if it just drains away in the pipe so easily this way without even a trace?

It is always delighted to see that there are so many multinational companies are generous to invest their resources in training and educating local Chinese people as it is crystal clear that majority of the Chinese people will be benefited from the process itself day after day. But such enthusiasm will not carry on if the results of most of these trainings cannot live up to the expectation of the program owners. The failure of many training programs of this kind might partially be attributed to an over-estimation of the readiness of their Chinese employees to catch up with the company's requirements through such trainings.

If it is fair to say that they may actually need more basic or elementary trainings before they are introduced to some sophisticated contents, it is my strong opinion that disappointing results out of these trainings could be more attributed to the inflexibility in designs of the programs and fuzziness in goal setting by the companies themselves in the first place.

I would personally tend to believe that Chinese people are more likely to better obtain new knowledge, absorb new ideas, acquire new skills by way of 'coaching' method instead of that they are locked up in a classroom for hours. A training by way of lecture in a classroom, however is hardly appealing to most Chinese staff, even though the trainer might try hard to enrich his class with lively elements like role-play, group discussion, case study, in addition to audio-visual teaching aids. Someone may argue that nowadays the younger generations of Chinese managers and staff have been through years of their school days for years and they should be supposed to get well used to the similar approach. After all, seldom have he ever heard any story of that his Chinese sub-ordinates would rise objection to or complaint on the class they are sent to. The fact that the majority of the Chinese people are relatively reserved in their personalities would mislead the top management in this regard. No complaints from a Chinese would probably be a sign of his compromising himself instead.

In contrast to the low effectiveness in training programs held in classroom, from my personal experiences it would be noticeably amazing to realize how many Chinese managers could devotedly learn advanced skills so briskly on his job when he is personally guided and coached on a daily basis by an experienced senior manager, instead of being fed with lectures and loaded up with literatures two days a week every three months. A thoughtful dedicate training program with a pool of mentorship would be helpful to breed a sophisticated team of local Chinese for the growing business here in the future.

Besides, 'train the trainer' is what I think one of the few most appropriate training approaches in China to start with, considering its cost effectiveness, flexibility in alternation of training contents, its practical dimension of a workshop-like interaction and its capacity of mission carrying and problem solving. The most appealing element is its offering an opportunity to found a workshop-like environment where all the participants can present and discuss in details the problems they really encounter in their daily life. It would be the most common approach that would be taken by many global companies in China, as recommended by their own human resources consultants for its cost effectiveness and its indirect yet strong influences to the entire organization, if successfully implemented. Unfortunately many trainings of this type would turn out much less promising than an acceptable level, and it is mainly due to a poor execution of the training and an inconsiderate selection of participants. Your decision to offer your local Chinese staff more training cannot be a wrong one since you have to eventually build up your own local team to succeed the management responsibilities of your local business. Though, it demands your favor to your local staff blended with a deliberate executive development program of long range. The practice of the latter requires you a policy of foresightedness and thoroughness in maneuvering your human resources wisely with enough motivation tools. By doing so, you would be freed from nuisances and troubles like staff quitting your company right after training, contradictory objectives of different trainings and so on.

When the above mentioned are subject to continuous adjustment in the implementation process day after day, the key question in the very beginning is: whom you should pick to be the trainer-to-be and what pre-requisites they are supposed to possess. In short words, I would say interpersonal skills, leadership and team playing skills should be the top three criteria to short-list your candidate list, assuming lots of other attributes should be related directly to your recruitment policies to filter your local people already.

## Reward or punishment?

It is simple that one who makes mistakes should take the blames and another who makes contribution should be awarded somehow. And most people are inclined to believe in award rather than punishment. After all, the history of mankind would have been rewritten if mankind had evolved into a species that does not own basic instincts of greed and self-defense.

'I am just mistaken the total monthly turnover with one more zero before the decimal point, what is the big deal? Anyway, nobody reading the report would ever believe this month we could make a sales turnover ten times last month?'...

'Yeah, I forgot to remind the supplier to ship the first order of back labels one week earlier, but anyway they are now in the warehouse already, it is me who made this mistake, but who doesn't now and then?'...

'I just can't believe it happens to me, working overtime for two weeks and my boss just seems indifferent to my hardworking? It is so unfair!'...

'I've never taken a sick leave the past 5 years, and my boss dared to give me a rise of monthly salary of merely 5%!'...

Complaints like this are fired in the pantries during office hours and continued in the pub and dining place afterwards everywhere everyday. Rewards and punishments are probably the biggest concern your employees would ever have, instead of the deadline for the proposal, or the upcoming visits of the big bosses, or your company being one of the Fortune 500 companies the first time. And as said before, people prefer reward to punishment and their opinions must vary to large extent how to reason a reward or punishment. But one thing for sure is that one usually, if not definitely, believes that if someone should be rewarded for some reasons or other, it should be himself who deserves it; and if someone is to be blamed, it would be him because someone else is in search of a scapegoat.

Chinese people share the similar views with the rest of the world, except that they appear to express their stronger preference on reward over punishment as a golden rule of thumb to manage people. They very likely believe in that rewards are always better means to motivate people to do or not to do things while punishment is not a good instrument in the business world so it should not be enforced if not extremely necessary.

It is an interesting finding that when it sounds so apparent that Chinese people are accustomed in their long tradition to the norm of 'setting an example by punishing the punished to the others', and courses of punishment can be found everywhere in the staff manual, company directives, management guidelines, work procedures and so on, a typical Chinese manager would try his utmost to avoid exercising punishment of some kind in their business activities or daily management even when it is deemed necessary. As a result, most of the verbal and written rules and regulations of punishment are just kind of propaganda to remind people all dos and don'ts and its possible consequences, there are much less occasions where you will see or hear people in a Chinese-managed company get fired, laid off or dismissed for a too much serious mistake he just made or his incompetence shown on the job or so. A belief of collective accountability explains partly a higher tolerance level on inefficiency and ineffectiveness in standing up to the principles of reward and punishment in a correct manner.

There are not many solutions to improve your situation like these. An education program to correct the mass's attitudes in your organization and continuous internal promotion to diffuse the messages inside the company may be helpful, but the results might not be instantaneous. If you expect a quick dosage of medication to amend their attitudes, you had better on one hand make sure every persons are well informed of concerned policies and on the other hand, impose them strictly according to the book whenever applicable under all circumstances in the very beginning. A swift decision and instant course of firm actions will serve a clear signal, if not too much a warning, to your people there is no room for substandard performance or fooling around in your leadership.

It should not ever be a worry from a good team of management that firing a lazy or irresponsible staff would portray an image of cruelty and cold-heartedness on you. Instead, you are supposed to worry about how to do it in compliance with the local labor laws and have the fired compensated reasonably according to the book of corporate guideline. It is not a matter of that you should abuse this here in China by taking advantage of the loopholes of needed-be-amended Chinese labor laws, because it is only your illusion that labor laws in China are loose and ill-executed everywhere so they possibly fail to protect their working citizens in the workplace. Foreign investments are not in a position to enjoying any privileges in this area, if not as a matter of fact that they are 'discriminated' expectedly to take up more responsibilities in conformation to the respective laws and rules with their utmost than some local state enterprises or smaller entrepreneurs.

# Local Chinese is inept at negotiation

In the business circles there have been some inside stories that foreign investments had taken advantage of Chinese people's ignorance in common principles of capitalism, unfamiliarity in international trading, inexperience in negotiation with foreign investments and so forth. Surely there have been some good deals closed with their local Chinese partners in big favor to the foreign investors. It had been a big and tough lesson learned by Chinese state government throughout the past 20 years.

Chinese government has been alert to this and top-down instructions are circulated and circulated again to all local governmental authorities from time to time to re-affirm the necessity of protecting the best interest of the nation and securing state owned assets and capitals under all circumstances. And they have been learning quickly and seemingly done a good job here in the past few years.

China has exhausted huge efforts to transform many state owned enterprises into public listed companies as core part of their economic reform in their 15-year national plan with a view to optimizing the capitalization and operation of their formerly state owned enterprises. But even a formerly state owned enterprise goes public in the legitimate manner; it does not mean that it is no longer stated owned or state run. The main difference is now they can outsource funding from the capital market in the public, but the controlling stake is still in the same hands and so is the decision making power. It is exactly what Mr. Zhu Rong-ji, the Prime Minister of People's Republic of China, was telling in the press conference after the 16th National Conference in March of 2001 that the reform in progress on state owned enterprises is not a privatization, as easily misunderstood by many westerners, it is a means to revitalize the enterprises by going public and yet the state is still the major shareholders of these enterprises after they go public in the stock market. And as described by Mr. Zhu, it can be said the ongoing progress is impressive and it develops in the right direction.

## An example of unprepared expansion

As a result, nowadays when foreign investment is looking for business co-operation or partnership with local corporations in China, you are still looking into a list of state owned or run enterprises in nature. You are probably going to meet the same old group of management of your prospective life-long partner(s) who dictated the company in a mind of socialistic mentality and a way of plan driven economists' for fifteen years and now steer the 'face-lifted' company with a hardship of fitting themselves into a world of languages of capitalism.

You rushed in should-to-shoulder with your competition with a high hope that you will defeat your competition as if you were the only one ready to triumph in this new world of virgin lands and tap the demand successfully. In the past decade since disassembling of Soviet Union, Russia, East Europe and especially China would have been the most frequent names appearing in your company newsletters or the hottest topics being talked about in the office. Your rivalries have been actively in search of new opportunities in these glittering new markets.

The company I worked for 7 years was starting its export business of its imported consumer brands into Russia through a local trader soon after the dismantling of Soviet Union in 1989. The business went steadily but never was close to drawing any attention or interest from the top management. Until it was 1993 or so they started up its own official distribution in association with a local partner as sole distributor for the whole product range then it worked some wonders somehow. The initial annual sales skyrocketed in millions by three times its value of re-export year on year basis. All indicators showed positive signs of big market potential, huge sales turnover and promising brand awareness. 2 years later an aggressive proposal on overseas acquisition was made to the board of directors and approved subsequently by the top management committee that a joint-venture company was to be founded in co-operation with the same distributor to oversee the sales and marketing functions locally. The following year such decision was awarded with an annual sales turnover of the first year 3 times the previous year.

The blue-sky picture remained for 2 years until in the third year all of a sudden the business neared dramatically to a deadly position with a titanic deviation from the yearly plan, and the projection made in the feasibility study. Everyone was panicked and most of them backed off to deny their involvement into this disaster by all means. For those who failed to slip away from the troubles, could only sleep with this headache every night and hope tomorrow would never come, if things would not get better in shape. Problems of various kind emerged and all these resulted in weaker and weaker financial position. Figures went south dreadfully, except that accounts receivables kept soaring to the record level. Cost saving was reinforced to re-shape the company's financial status, new products were launched to boost up the sales turnover, more advertising and promotions were executed to recover shelf off-take, but all in vain like a shoot in the dark. Less than two years later the joint-venture company was announced its death by liquidation.

Long after the wound healed, people started to realize that the whole project would be died of a lack of thoughtful planning, reckless implementation of the plan, and most importantly, partnering with the wrong partner.

It would be some similar stories that you would hear from your peers in the industries now and then in China, except that most of the victims are clinging to the last hope that the situation would improve if they remain patient as they are now. Most stories in China will never end because most of the big shoots from foreign investments see China a market different enough from Russia to justify their decision to go on investing instead of de-investment even though their current businesses are dragging on alike. There are 1.3 billions people over there and you make a fortune if collecting 1 RMB from everyone of them once. The mathematical calculation sounds very tempting and you do not need a rocket scientist or brain surgeon to confirm it. Moreover, there are in the real world some successful encouraging examples of other companies that you read in the flight magazines or just overheard the last time. That is good enough to refresh your mind and brainwash you with fascinating dreams.

## Partnership fallen apart

When investment into China became a heat wave hitting the international big players of various industries 10 years ago, some pioneers did work some magic from scratch. They were exploring this nation of unknown world by trial and error but succeeded in standing on their own feet eventually. Though, they had hovered for age in the very beginning before they would have a kick-off.

Initiating your feasibility study in investment in China, you were to deal with many poker-faced governmental officials, and hopefully, if your company name could ring a bell, you would be recommended some potential local partners with which you could consider to co-operate in form of joint venture establishment. Immediately you will be deeply impressed by the enthusiasm and warm hospitality over thrown to you by these potential partners in the first meeting with each of them by ways of sightseeing tour and one banquet after another. If you are skillful enough, you might redirect your dialogue on the business topics half an hour out of visitation for the whole day, collecting some plain information and figures hand-written in rough sheets, if not purely verbally.

After rounds of courteous visit, you are closing in to one of them for a serious business negotiation. You are not alone in the whole process of individual negotiation with your counterpart, because you again were dealing with a crowd of general manager and his team of deputies, accompanied with a bunch of government officials from all kinds of authorities. In order to strike a deal with the best favorable terms and conditions, you strive to lobby with each one of them for another favorable terms on exemption on taxation, use of land, importing machineries, and so on.

Chinese people have their own mysterious way to present business figures that is either unknown or inconceivable to most foreign investment. The business figures presented by the Chinese counterpart are always ill formatted and incomparable to international standards in accounting or finance, and in many cases you would be shocked at the aggressiveness in their projection of sales trend and the profitability of the would-be joint venture. For so many reasons you would have to keep your doubts on the raw data on which the mouth-watering projection on sales and profitability would be based with yourselves. With the negotiation zigzagging too long already, many foreign investors are compelled to take the risk and would just go on walking in the thin line. Anyway, you need them to blueprint your feasibility study and finalize your strategic papers for submission to the board in the next board meeting.

For three months surrounded by a crowd of high-ranking officials, making endless acquaintances with faceless officials on countless banquets and parties and meetings, you take eventually a big leap forward addressing all the pending issues with your partner and the authorities. Legal papers fly and talks talked and calls made for another three months. After the big bosses flew 4,000 miles over and met face-to-face with the same group of local people from the other side of the fence, a memorandum to mark the establishment of the new joint venture is signed finally. From the board, the green light is later granted from and the deal is ultimately closed. Needless to say, there will be another big signing ceremony followed by a big banquet for 120 persons whom 70% of them you never met before then and 95% you would never meet again since then.

When it is assumed the toughest time has been over and it is time to roll up sleeves and get down to business, you would immediately find that there is another round of negotiation waiting for you. And it is probably the phase of a real negotiation.

Most people would think one's exposure and experiences in international environments would enrich to certain extent his abilities and capabilities of handling negotiations. It is just like a soldier who fought a real war before and survived it should have expectedly learned gradually how to fight a battle wisely without getting himself killed, at least not by a chain of naïve thoughts and course of silly actions during the fight. It applies to our business world by most people at the top and therefore they would jump a little too quick to a conclusion that Chinese businessmen would very likely be less experienced than westerners when business negotiations are conducted, since China has been clammed up for so many year before it started to get in touch massively to the 'major' western world around 20 years ago. Hence, a majority of westerners would associate Chinese people with conservative thinking, ignorance and naïveté, and naturally under-estimate their capabilities in handling business negotiations and assume falsely that they would be masterfully out-smarted if done purposely and carefully.

A trial on doing so will end up with a big surprise. We should not forget how tough it had been for Chinese people to build up their nation as of today by defending themselves from invasions, then surviving various social movements and political turbulence the past decades. It can be said Chinese people of nowadays are also trained up in its own way to ready themselves to every kind of challenges ahead on various matters in every area, from daily lives to international matters. Who thinks that way ought to work harder on his second thought before he is going to take advantage of this illusionary assertion, or it would be himself who is going to pay the price.

## Repetitive negotiations

With a signed and sealed agreement on hand, you think things cannot get worse and what you need is some more time and patience to clear and clarify. So you started your negotiation again and assume it has to be easier since there is already a written agreement as a platform of common ground for further communication. The truth is that you and your colleague will be disappointed. Before the signing it is the Chinese side who would be pushy in the project, and after a grand signing ceremony they will resume into a mode of slow motion especially when you are anxious to speed up things as agreed formerly.

What was written in the legal papers you collected so far for the deals could be referred from time to time when either side of the partnership initiate any further discussions. But most Chinese partners as yours would just think that most of these official documents are there for reference only and they are simply useless and therefore are not worth a reference check in them. The legal spirit would assume that both sides to abide by the agreement entered, but Chinese people have a slightly different perspective on legal terms and conditions stipulated in pages after pages in the so-called agreements or contracts from the western world, unfortunately.

If you observe closely enough your partner, read carefully the contracts you have collected for the past five years, or recall your meetings that you have gone to for legal matters, you may conclude there are some common understanding and views on legal stuffs borne in many Chinese people's mind.

Firstly, when westerners tend to believe legal papers produced in the business is the most civilized way to make clear statement on the rights and responsibilities and obligations of whoever are entering into that contract and it is beyond doubt that what they say or do on the subjects is bound to these clauses afterwards. Therefore this book of doctrine is always lengthy as needed, covering most if not all the possible probabilities a human brain could ever imagine, magnifying its scope as widest as possible, as thorough and elaborative as one term defined in hundred words in 3 languages and etc.

Chinese people also accept it as civilized, but certainly not the most. A lengthy contract of more than 3 pages sounds not only lengthy but also superfluous to them and therefore a mere formality for the sake of a completeness of a business deal. They give their respects to the legal documents because they see it as a gesture to give respect to their guests, not the legal spirit itself reflected in each word imprinted in the documents.

Secondly, westerners think that legal document is power. A contract like this is always adored as the highest, even after the expiration of such contract one is supposed to live in its shield for his interest, when someone else in its shadow. Whenever necessary, they are more than pleased to refer to this 'bible of the dos and don'ts' and quote from it to protect their interests every working day. Sometimes together with a twisted interpretation it just gets the job done. It is the body armor to defense your interests, and your weapon as well just in case.

Chinese people instead would follow their distinctive perceptions on purpose of contract and agreement and basically put them at the bottom of their drawers once they are signed and sealed. To them, it is merely a written record of what had been said and agreed and so they can just simply talk about it again should there raise up any subject of dispute in common concerns. A second look at the contract by the very same Chinese in a different place at a different time would inspire you with a different interpretation on the specific clauses. It does happen in China.

Thirdly, a contract or agreement if drafted by a western legal practitioner ought to have precisely exhausted in calculated manner, the rights, responsibilities and obligations entitled by the entering parties respectively. More importantly, in addition to its plain but yet clear attribute of summarizing the deal over the business negotiation, an agreement can be, in plain words, translated into a complete checklist of dos and don'ts and it simply serves to describe to all the entering parties clearly and entirely what the forthcoming courses of actions should be. They are perceived as a mandate and should be strictly followed. It is the basic philosophy of a legal agreement or contract.

However, Chinese people have a tendency to treat a legal agreement a written repetition of what has been promised to do by parties respectively. As a result, you see more often the 'dos' instead of the 'don'ts' in a typical agreement among the Chinese, and the latter is often subconsciously left as unspoken verbal agreement. As a result, a Chinese would follow 'partially' the agreement and do what he is obliged to do as clearly defined on the paper, and in the meantime, he would decide at his discretion if he would or would not do whatever is not mentioned at all.

The last but not least, Chinese people tend to prefer some reasonable ambiguities in sensitive areas under all circumstances and expect a future resolution by both parties' effort, and patience, when westerners are used to rigorously define in scary legal terms and exhaust everything in black and white on the paper. Without a nod from their nicely paid legal advisor, most things, if not all, will be hanged in the air. To downplay any disagreement stuck in the process and suffer from a hanging to-be-closed deal forever, Chinese party can 'reasonably' give in and have the negotiation moved on to the final and the easiest step, for the sake of a harmonious relationship and a bright future.

Despite of that on many occasions Chinese people would still share the respect of westerners on legal spirit sparkled in all legal document, they are clear-minded enough to remind themselves of their own version of interpretation on each clause spelled out in the paper and are more than willingly to remind you as well in case some dispute of various scales occurs.

All these discrepancies in perception of what an agreement in black and white is for produce loopholes and leave room for misunderstanding and misinterpretation among the parties, which would eventually spoil the deal and a bright future of the joint-venture company.

## *Can never mend a ruined relationship*

You have the same question spinning in your head that is what the causes would be to your problems on hand, downward sliding sales turnover month after month, quality issues on new product development, monthly cash flow running out, and a 24-hour surveillance from your boss by long-distance calls, a bunch of officials from local authorities chasing after you for unknown reasons…and worst of all, your Chinese partner refuses to talk to you any longer in the meantime. This puzzle has become part of your life. You are paid to live with it, but before long you start to wonder if you get paid enough for this torture…

It is almost an art concerning how to downplay the done damage and take remedy measures of damage control in the business in China, especially when it comes to a ruined relationship with Chinese people. If you think it is a matter of patience and time for several thorough communications with an openness of heart-felt assurances to amend, you will be more dying to knowing why it does not happen the way you anticipate. Even when it happens that way, it may not home in where you expect things will improve for you or your company.

In a dispute with your Chinese partner, you may dissociate the persons to whom you are talking with his company that you are accusing with its failure to deliver its promises. That is why most the times when a dispute arises in between, you start with an opening remark of 'don't take it personal' followed with what you really mean to say about the business. A frequent repetition of such in the entire process of hot discussion is deemed to be the basic manner to show that your respect to him as an individual does not diminish even you are actually yelling at him for the entire meeting. Of course you might not think so when you two would switch role for a minute. It is a rule of thumb to behave in a business meeting disguising your true feeling and emotions, and think and talk and do in business-like fashion whenever is necessary.

This manner is also well rooted in the minds of Chinese businessmen and some of them can imitate as good as many westerners. After all, many Chinese people have made it a habit disguising their feelings and emotions for so many years and they do not mind doing it again for a good reason. But a Chinese would tend to associate you and your team with their company behind very closely. It explains very easily why a personal connection or so-called 'Guangxi' in China can spell magic much more dramatically than you might see in the west.

Now you are suffering from a ruined relationship with your Chinese partner when the joint-venture company is dragging on and zigzagging to nowhere in sight. You get calls from your right-hand man, the general manager of this infant business in China, complaining how the Chinese-party-appointed deputy general manager is doing lousy production plan for the past three months and that the chairman of the Chinese company has refused to co-operate on speeding up its capital injection as promised and the expatriate sales director is pressing him to hire him a company chauffer and etc.

You immediately send your second-in-command there to cool down the whole situation but his tone on the phone sounds as depressed as the general manager after 3 months in this mess. What else can be done has been done and there is no light of future in sight to relieve your stress.

There is nothing for sure except that if your man has done something to ruin the relationship, you should not hold high hope that the same person can amend it on his own. The advice from me is to side-line him or get him replaced, at least for a certain period of time, so get someone new to pamper the partners. As said before, Chinese people take thing personal and therefore it is difficult to restore a relationship with someone they already have a bad feeling with. Unless you are not in a hurry on the business, you need a new face to impress your partner as a starting. It is not a strong dose to throttle your business at high speed, but at least you can have a chance to resume the mutual communications. Whether the situation will be improved then depends on whom you have picked, if he is the right messenger to remedy the situation.

## *Sidelining the wrong guys*

The most secure way should be to establish and maintain a constant and thorough communications with your Chinese partner. It is the fundamental element to grow mutual understanding. A channel of rumor-proof communication and open-minded understanding costs you little and does you no harm in times of peace, and it does do you a lot of good at tough times.

Of course it is assumed you have picked the right persons to look after your and your company's relationship with your Chinese partner. After all, it is only that 'people' as an element matters in the real world, other than some people with the money and power.

A good negotiator and lobbyist should pay no less attention to what a Chinese has said and given a comment on the subjects on various occasions, no matter how subtle it might sound, other than what clauses are written in a legal document on which some signatures can be found. It is too risky to take it light-hearted in the verbal communications and all likely meanings of each verbal statement and comment and it would be deadly for a foreign investor to take for granted for what is written on the paper.

Whenever the alarm blasts its way back to you that someone in your team turns out to be a 'troublemaker' rocking the boat so much that your Chinese partner is unwillingly annoyed about him, it is your discreet consideration and judgment on whether and how to sandbag him or sideline him, for enough time, to safeguard not only the other crews, but also the whole business. It would be otherwise only if the troubles he is making are intentionally in your master plan, as some situations would require. You had better not ever expect the same troublemaker would compose himself again in a shape, which would impress and comfort your Chinese partner somehow and make right the relationship again.

Besides, your legal advisor is there to alert you for any possible legal advices you may be in need of and you should expect not more than that. Not an interpreter, not an entertainer, not even someone who should be in the frontier of the negotiation field if not necessary. A low-key legal advisor will always be better than one who packs in his attaché case hundreds of legal questions in written form and ready to throw them brutally to your partner in the faces every single minute. The worst scenario would be that your legal consultant is tempted not to miss some good chances to simulate the negotiation table to a court and start 'cross examining' your poor Chinese partner.

# Language is the biggest barrier

Everyone feels uneasy facing an unknown environment where you understand none of what the others say or write. Anxieties inside you gradually rule your responses and manipulate your decisions accordingly. How to keep a clear and calm mind is one of the tough questions for foreign investors when they are about to venture into a strange world on the other side of the world since it enables them to make good judgment and right decisions day by day.

International trading has been driving business people into almost every corner to materialize potentials ahead. Traveling overseas is no longer a nightmare since you either have made it out of a habit or quitted this long time ago, willingly or unwillingly. Now and then in your whole career time, you fly to and fro continents and land on foreign cities for a stay of two days or a decision of million's worth.

Meeting your business associates and partners, you are happy with your gift of language as it lets you know what is going on in these strange places. You even enjoy sometimes speaking their language with accent, reading their local sports news in the newspapers, and even chatting with the bartender in the pub. Your ability to do so gives you a sense of security and an appeal to explore the city more deeply next time. Your ability to finally making a strange place a home away from home to yourself would be nice experiences, however, it is not easy in China, as you might in other Asian countries where English is well received by the majority of local people.

## An adventure to an unknown world

So when you were first told to pack your luggage and belongings and your secretary passed to you a single air ticket to China, you might have a little doubt on how such an ancient country would look like and even your mind was slightly drifted away by recalling its tourist spots you saw in the postcard. Anyhow you were anxious to see it yourself and hopefully you can survive a plain life style for two years or so until you would be called back to the headquarters with a promotion up the ladder after some impressive performance across the ocean.

You must still recall your arrival of the first time in China after 15 hours of air travel, it was only when your flight taxied at the airport in Shanghai and stepped on the land of unknown, you could fail to find the right exit to baggage claim since hardly was there any legible directory in English in the so-called international airport. When you were bullying shoulder-to-shoulder with local people at the taxi stand, you could not help starting to get worried about your surviving your daily life in this 'lousy' place. The challenges in your assignment could be minimal if you even could not ever get a ride to the hotel…

Having labored to settle down in the city, you thought you were young enough to pick up a foreign language, at least some basic simple words for daily communications in addition to some simple characters so you can read at least the nameplate of the street hoisted by the roadside. Only your effort was a waste of time to you two months later when you gradually understand how many dialects there are in China and how likely a Chinese would speak his dialect instead of the official Mandarin that you would only hear in the evening news in the television. The Chinese characters are not less horrible when you come to that. Four weeks spent and you could only read the Chinese characters for number one to number ten and your tutor would suggest you to work harder as if you did not.

In the office you were more than happy with that many of your local staff could speak simple English and some of them fluent enough to entertain you with some dirty jokes at coffee break sometimes. And those filled in the senior positions were all graduated from famous local universities, spent some time studying abroad and then returned with a MBA so you just felt like yourself at home with them in an evening gathering or causal talk. However, when you think that you will be problem free handling the business the way you are used in the head-quarters, it turns out to be a different story at all. Because you are smart enough to remind yourself that one mistranslation or misunderstanding would cost your hundred thousands and therefore you had better watch out when you get down to business with your staff, colleague, and most important of all, your clients and business partners. It would be a very painful adventure full of daily stress and pressure.

Thanks gods you have some senior local staff who appear speaking fluent English here and it is time to better utilize the company's resources. It sounds a good idea that from now on when you get to visit your business acquaintances, you will bring along one of them and have him playing an interpreter for you lest something would happen to embarrass your or the company or your guests.

You need a right-hand man to act as your personal interpreter. A good interpreter can then help you to walk through some thin ices everyday and sustain your control over the daily business by feeding you with bits and pieces of information from which you are blocked by a barrier of language. In fact, your career in China is more or less cling-ing to the availability of a good interpreter and his abilities to keep pace with you in the works.

## Interpreter is no amateur

Most people may possess a perception that language barrier should be in favor of those who can communicate in the most commonly accepted language: English, because most business activities are being concluded everywhere in the world in the language of English day by day. It must be admitted beyond any doubt that English is and will still be the one and only one real international language on earth, which people of different nationalities could communicate and do business and build up mutual relationship eventually.

In general it gives people an impression that East Asia is the region around the Pacific Rim where you might find more difficulties in communicating in English with the local people since there are more people who fails to command any English than elsewhere and I think it is not a false statement. And such a statement might have to be an understatement to describe the current situation in China.

Specifically speaking, due to the fact that English is so dominating in the business world, a foreign businessman who possesses a good command of English with a group of English native speaking assistants is supposed to take advantage of their language ability and consequently dominate in their business negotiations with local Chinese businessmen, who are just few examples out of the population of billions who cannot technically speak or understand any foreign language at all. It is fair to say nowadays there are still a lot of Chinese people would be thrilled when they are asked some kinds of plain question in English in the street and you could immediately see their feeling of inferiority crawl all over their faces. In this aspect, foreign investments seem to be compensated with some advantages, technically and psychologically in this strange land. But it is only one side of the coin and the other side will not be so encouraging to many foreign investments.

There are still ways to iron out the barrier of language. A profession called 'interpreter' could do the jobs for you. Unfortunately in China seldom can you meet some professional interpreters active in business sector and there are few of them involved in working for the real big foreign corporations investing in China, for some reasons or the other.

Hence, what the foreign investments are doing to overcome the barrier is mostly picking up an amateur interpreter and having him or her sent to the occasion where an interpreter is needed, badly. And the most economical and convenient choice is right sitting somewhere inside the company. The secretary to general manager, that lady assistant to marketing manager, the regional sales manager or Miss. bookkeeper would be one of the choices available. They can be easily qualified for the job if they are able translate some key words from English to Mandarin and vice versa in the office, they definitely can in the management meeting, at least the management would think they are, regardless of the importance of the topics on hand.

Here comes the show time. It would be stunned that in a top management meeting reviewing the current business situation, directors and controllers all around the long table are strangely nodding their heads mercifully when a young lady you later recognize as the assistant manageress in marketing department, criticizing in her own words the poor performance of the company and accusing sales director of his inability to place the new products on shelves of 90% of the key account and etc. in front of the Chinese attendants…and very soon the dialog may turn out to be between the lady and the sales director without a chance to let any English speaking managers poke their ears in the arguments…

As you can imagine, in many cases half of what should be translated is left untouched or ill translated between the Chinese and foreigners when the discussion is getting hotter. You may not be happy to learn two months later that your messages were not conveyed to the attendants thoroughly and completely, not even modestly and therefore damages are done to the operations. A meeting like this could deter the management team from discussing daily issues constructively and effectively, let alone to grant them the occasions to reach agreement or make consensual decisions.

A distortion in communication among core members by ill translation could cause severe damage and interferences on your daily operating business. Any intentional attempt to mislead the management by ill translation would lay a time bomb in your company since it would only propel your company into a state of catastrophe-like crisis in misunderstanding among the management. When the heat gets to trigger the bomb, there would be a war of paper among departments, or worse comes to the worst, a truckload of accusation and legal papers between you and your Chinese partners.

How many meetings have you witnessed ended with hot discussions and name calling at one another? A failure to ally all the people in the same boat will be just the beginning of a years-long nightmare to a short-lived organization.

The only way to avoid unnecessary misunderstanding among your people is to set up a mechanism to deal with all communications and translation by professionals. When most of your staff appear to striving for a chance to show you his or her excellent command of foreign language and how helpful he or she can be to lend you a hand in talking to your Chinese partner, it is always a wise idea to equip you and your team with a capable and objective interpreter all the way along. Once you and your company could buy this idea and I promise you that you will later find it a wise move. And it is especially a good move to shield your team from unnecessary chaos in daily operations.

## Read and listen between the lines

You come from another English speaking country or you have been speaking English most the times you travel overseas. It is no surprise to you that your daily communications in China need to be completed with Chinese-back translation of some kinds by somebody else. You might have been alerted a necessity of companying with a good translator wherever you are in China, even halting a taxi in the street. Keeping him a company reachable at arm's length can save you from many troubles. And you are satisfied with his proficiency in English and his performance dealing with your Chinese partner so far.

Everything works just fine with your interpreter, until you start picking up calls from your Chinese partner or receiving written reports for the same subject matters continuously. Meeting after another among the concerned parties have been hosted but to an avail as your Chinese partner keeps coming back to you for the same questions. You are totally pinned down to the same matters no matter how patient you let yourself be.

Being used to communicate in English with people of alternate mother tongue in Asia, western businessmen have a tendency to totally rely on what is translated back in English words and terms when processing the messages by the usual meaning of those words. Many of them actually are taking a risk of missing one important word or misunderstanding the subtle meaning of particular phrase in the entire discussion. If otherwise, a decision might have been altered on your side and things would have gone more smoothly. Even a top grade interpreter in the field cannot help. They are simply left no single chance to try to listen 'between' the words or reading 'between' the lines from your Chinese partner or colleague.

The price would be very high, as everyone can imagine. And especially Chinese are likely some people who prefer subtle expressions on their opinions or viewpoints, and it is even more or less a phenomenon that the more critical the subjects are in discussion, the more subtle their expressions are to be.

A Chinese would say 'yes' when he actually is saying 'I will consider it' or he might say 'no' just with the same implication as 'I will consider it'. Chinese people are trained by its long histories to perform skillfully in his unique way in a negotiation or business discussion. Being isolated from the outside world for so long does not make them a fool when talking about a business deal of millions' worth. You must keep your concentration on your Chinese partner whenever important topics are on the table for both sides, their body language, their gesture, the facial expression, and learn to rely less on your interpreter or translator's verbal translation if you desire to get to know your Chinese partner.

### Reliable legal advisor

It is also a very interesting phenomenon that hardly will you meet professional interpreters on many occasions where serious business negotiations are taking place. Instead, you find that the 'interpreters' sitting next to the big bosses actually are marketing manager, sales director or so. The less unfortunate cases would be that a lawyer plays interpreter, at least a lawyer is supposed to be more cautious when they are talking, especially on behalf of their clients. My advice to you is to give a serious consideration on hiring an in-house interpreter to facilitate your daily communication with your key Chinese staff and make sure there is no communication breakdown between your team and your Chinese partners, and the officials from governmental authorities. In the meantime, you must be willing to open up yourself to overcome the barrier of language and cultivate a mutual understanding between both parties.

Your casualness in mindset, total dependence on your interpreter, and too strong belief in written agreement could poison you and your team when dealing with Chinese people in serious business.

Most business starts with a negotiation. Here one's personal experiences make him big difference from an average negotiator to a professional one. As a foreigner coming to China for the first time, one who can open up his mind to foreign culture and respect it is likely in a better position in founding a firmer platform on which he interacts with his Chinese counterparts. You do not need a gift from god to read people's minds so you can better understand your Chinese partners, instead you need more patience and open-mindedness at the very beginning and when you learn the tricks, it will earn you and your team the respect and friendship from your Chinese partners and spare you from irreversible troubles with them.

# Big country plus big population equals to big demand

It has long been an attraction to the foreigners that China is such a big and ancient country in this planet. Unfortunately its attractiveness has brought to it not many good old memories. The country's modern histories in turmoil for the past century has left many Chinese people an attitude of hostility towards western world.

Massive invasions and colonization by foreign nations for decades, followed by the excruciating experiences in the years of World War II intercepted with years of civil war…all these jammed together torturing the Chinese people for almost a century before it came to rest on a state where social disorder and anxieties of life was somehow replaced by a future full of hopes and prosperities. This fate can be ascribed to the fact that China is such a boundless land of exploited gigantic resources and not many foreign countries would leave it untouched before reach it with a handful of resources of all kind, by some means.

If it is correct that some economists were saying the fall of Great Britain empire was a result of its exhaustion of own resources in their homeland and at the same time failing to stop its United Kingdom from dissolving decades before, it would somewhat explain the fate of China in its sheer aching experiences with the west the past centuries.

Centuries ago it was kind of invasions and colonization by force to clear up the entrance to this land, and now along with the civilization of mankind, new approaches are adopted and efforts of invasion are diverted into the boundary of trade and industry in the country. This time, China itself would be benefited to greater extent in a sense of modernization of the country and acceleration of improvement on living standard of the Chinese people.

It has been a very tempting statement in the past and still echoing in the air when a foreign investor first comes to a decision of expanding its foothold into this country, and it does not require you a rocket scientist to explain the vast market potential in the eye of most businessmen who are at present looking under the rock for every opportunity to grow their businesses an inch ahead. Apparently, 1.3 billions of population in China and a slice of this potential would equate a tidy sum in the annual report of the company. Furthermore, it does hardly sound a rather remote and therefore unreachable dream if you are going to capture this market wisely and ahead of your competition.

Hearing this, some conservative thinkers might try to calm down their heads from this exciting idea and start to analyze the situation by his business acumen. However meticulous they might be, this idea appears still very much appealing even they come to reason by a perspective of pragmatism, the fact that only tenth of the whole population would afford and be willing to give patronages to their products or services in a year would result in a big leap forward for their businesses. As if bewildered at winning a lottery of millions suddenly, additional sales turnover of 130 millions is yet a very nice figure to sleep with, assuming one could succeed to make a sale of one dollar's worth from this one-tenth of entire population in China.

Serious strategic business review meetings are called for and followed by a series of hardworking studies and well-laid plans to blueprint the building of the biggest than ever bridgehead in the east.

Only when the machineries turn into motion and your local troops are mobilized for few months, the infant business starts to skew off track from the plan month after month. The figures in the reports begin to intimidate some big bosses in the headquarters and furrow some others' eyebrows. The heat is on and more up-coming bad news further arouses more and more questioning attention from the board of directors or major shareholders. Less than two years their patience will finally evaporate in hopelessness and the start-up business would then be left unattended to struggle on its own.

Is it that difficult to collect 1 RMB from each of tenth of the total population in this country to make a fortune for the company when you did witness Chinese people generously spending their hard-earned money on a Big Mac or a latest model of Nokia mobile phone, out of their monthly income of 800RMB or so? What secret spell is missing in your nice local business operation to trigger their patronage to your internationally famous branded product, which you are confident that its features can excel most of the competition, from domestic market or abroad?

## China as a developing country

Various statistics published by the National Statistics Bureaus on economic development in China or advancement of living standards for Chinese people have been very pleasing and encouraging not only to the central government but also lots of foreign investments. The government sees their relentless effort be rewarded when foreign investors can smell the market potentials inside the data. Ranging from the ratio of number of telephone lines versus total population to the ever growing GDP per capita, from the literacy rate of its people to the growth rate of foreign trade per year, all the figures pinpoint to more or less one conclusion: the economic growth is heading to the unprecedented high level and not a signal of slow-down or so is remotely foreseen.

Yet China is still a developing country though some people cannot accept this fact for some political reasons or other. Regardless of the fact that some statistics are presenting to you a very promising market potential in Chinese market and strong consumption power and relatively high disposable income of its people, the width of the gap between the rich and the poor is extremely big and results in polarizing the consumption power of the people in few big coastal cities and those in the inland regions.

People in few rapidly rising cities in coastal provinces are getting rich and their disposable incomes are increasing proportionally. Their desires to upgrade their standards of living are unquestionable and observable in the past years. Though most of these people in these cities on the rise are still far from the entry level of which they can dispose their income at the will freely on some 'luxury' goods. If taking a closer look at the statistics released by the government, someone probably cannot help scratching his head finding out the average monthly income for a citizen in working class in Shanghai at around RMB600. As Shanghai is always claimed as the 'dragonhead' city leading the whole nation to the forthcoming prosperous years ahead, one may base on this to outline a closer-to-reality picture of the market.

China is a wagon that needs more horsepower than it has right now to throttle its wheels and requires as well a mastermind to steer it. One ought not to be oblivious at its truckloads of burdens, the uncertainties of on-going economic reforms on economy, the huge population dependent on the country's well-being, the agonizing re-engineering of the public administrations, and etc. One careless mistake might drive it off the track and the international world might have to suffer the consequences one way or the other economically and politically, to certain extent.

It is always delighted for businessmen to do business in a booming market, but it does not mean all the business will accordingly get booming the next day. The minority of particular businesses and industries will flourish before most of the others as demand in certain products or services in the market will usually grow first.

It is no surprise that in the past a white-collar could collect his daily necessities from his workplace like soap, toothpaste and so forth as part of his fringe benefit. Time flies and now he is compensated twice as much as he was 5 years ago, and he can afford to buy his daily necessities in the supermarket. Now he has a choice, whether he continues to collect his soap and washing powder each season in his workplace or he buys them at his discretion his preferred brands in the market. Even he can now afford to get some nicer ones himself, he may not prefer buying at his own expense. Perhaps his wife succeeds convincing him the benefits of a better quality soap offered in the market, he has still a variety of local or imported brands to choose from. A serial process of decision-making is expected in a consumer before it finally is transformed into a demand, and the more the number of processes there are, the less possibility it turns out to be an ascertained demand on YOUR products.

In a market where the majority of the consumers are distracted to fulfilling more basic needs of their own, a headline of 'Number of Ferrari sold in China set record high' in China Daily is not at all any good news to those who have invested their real money or are going to invest in here and expected to a reasonable rate of return on investment since the news itself fails to reflect the real picture of the market in general.

Unless your investment is not going to serve the mass market here, your may consider to make your business plan a more conservative one in order to 'play safe or pay with what is in your safe'.

## *Imparity of Wealth*

You are delighted to see so many Mercedes roam along the highways in Shanghai or Guangzhou or Beijing, and there are local Chinese behind the wheel most the times, not to mention the stocky Cadillac or sporty BMW around the corners. Everything in sight shows a booming market thirsty for branded goods of luxury and privileges everywhere.

What you see is the bright side of the country. As if you have no many choices when traveling in the country and probably you are, in Beijing you are always too busy in partying with high ranking officials to take a side look at the slum areas three blocks away; in Shanghai your scheduled stay too tight to pay a visit to the nearby counties or towns in the villages; in Guangzhou your meeting with local clients too lengthy in White Swan Hotel to register the picture of homeless street sleepers underneath the flyover; in Xi'an your sightseeing too inspiring to notice the closed-down stores along the street...

The situation of imparity of wealth is getting worse and it is worsening at an unbelievable pace. When the gap is getting wider, the worst is that there exists no as many opportunities as in the west for the poor to improve their lives in a proper manner. The chance to receive education in school for children in poverty is slim, social welfare for the poor is minimal, opportunities in career are limited, all these sum up to threaten the nation as a whole on its social stability. It has become one of the top priorities of the national administration's concern these years.

When you are projecting your business in the next five years in a bar chart with a basic assumption of ten millions of potential consumers striving to seize your products on shelves at a growth rate of 30% per year, you might be just misapprehending a fantasy far from the real world. Executing the plan may end you up with a wearisome business in its heavy deficit.

All in all, a projection of the demand from the local consumers should not be lightheartedly magnified in the light of the overwhelming population size of 1.3 billions and some gorgeous good-looking pictures of few cities in the heat, if it cannot be reasoned with plausible explanations.

## Cost of Sales

It is impressive to see a shiny Mercedes Benz cruising in the highway or a fleet of Audi and GM tripping in the heavy traffic in Shanghai, or business-looking executives striding in and out the five-star hotels in the commercial areas. You are convinced by these interesting findings that demand is right there and so are your opportunities. The answer is positive, but I am afraid the next question is far more important than this: how can you size up the demand and access to them?

The fact that more citizens can afford a Mercedes or more local companies afford to lease the whole floor in a well situated luxuriously furnished office complex is by all means good signs indicating the economy is heating up, confidence shared by the majority of the people around you is the fundamental to an economy. The question is whether there is enough demand you can just fit your products or services in fulfilling them, let alone whether there are actually substitutes from others readying to replace you at anytime.

The history of foreign investments participating in automobile industry in China could be one of the typical examples to describe how tragic it could be after an international player would have stepped into it domestic market at high profile and, very soon had their business heading nowhere.

Some of them are still struggling with its profit and loss statement every year, when some others are begging humbly for some more favorable policies to strengthen their position in the market. There are few others who are warning or threatening to withdraw from the market whereas some of them have neared to end up vanished as forced by the market through de-investing. Until the recent two years they start to see some lights glistering far ahead their long roads since there come first some manipulation on demand by the government and some favorable policies on promoting spending on automobile market.

Such dependence of your local business on the policies and regulations orchestrated in the hands of the administration was not the likes of capitalism in the west and therefore many foreign investments, if not all, are not able to waltz with them in carefree motion.

If it is not one thing, it is another. Enjoying the privileges in the city where they landed their investment, worse enough, they were taken by the scruff by local authorities of other cities and provinces when they were expanding their business across the border. Blunt notorious practice of trade protectionism by most local administrations on provincial and city level was like a civil war in economic terms and their big plans were practically announced a death. A business plan projecting a steady growth on nationwide demand on automobiles for the next ten to fifteen years had resulted in the start-up capital investment on production facilities and machineries too heavy to be justified by its extreme over-capacity afterwards, let alone a huge number of labors were taken over as requested. Return on investment would remain understandably unacceptable for the coming years, if not decades. Surely it is not a story that would only cast sour memories to the teeth of some automobile makers.

When many others are excitedly addicted to the statistics books published by various research groups or by the Chinese government itself, in which a blue-sky picture is described marvelously to attract as many foreign investors as possible, a wise businessman would consider at his second thought a more in-depth information collecting about the potential market. Substantial groundwork should be foreseen right from the beginning in the initial stage of conceptualization of an idea about business expansion or diversification. Opportunity cost is all it is required to explain this since you will see how different your company would look if you had invested the resources on the current business instead of a slippery business expansion in a totally new market. Only thorough and precise groundwork and planning can suffice to secure you with higher probability of future success and, supply you with some feasible alternatives should you be entrapped somewhere in the processes.

If a reliable and trustworthy market research reveals that specific demand in the market where you are targeting appears not so encouraging or so, you had better stay put for a while until more market variables are indicative of some positive signals. Early birds might get more food in the morning, though they would get easily killed by the long-waiting hunters as well.

After all, business environment and market situation everywhere in the world are so dynamic nowadays, it is like music chair for all the players and each of them can have their turns. Merciless as it is to investing in China, it does not matter any longer who comes first; the question of today is who will be served better.

## *In search of consumer*

Once there have been many theories in marketing to help you understand your customers. One of core elements in these theories is to make use of the data extracted from the marketing research to predict how likely your consumer will behave in their consumption and base on the conclusions to deploy your marketing strategies accordingly.

Though the predictability of your consumer behaviors today is not as straightforward as it was 10 years ago. In the former time it would have been sufficient if the market in focus was segmented by some criteria and you could just pick the right segment as your target. The pattern of their behaviors in that segment would therefore further be analyzed to draw you some conclusions on which your company would devise your strategies. Nowadays, the market is extremely diversified and a segmentation of market by certain criteria or pre-defined characteristics would fail to generate a reliable and clear-cut sub-market for you to work on. Even though your research team is capable of locating your target consumer in a concise and lucid description, their thinking and behavior would change day by day under such a dynamic environment before you are ready to 'capture' them by your hands.

For instance, brand loyalty was once a key element in marketing principles and everyone was working hard on creative marketing tools to either establish or maintain consumers' loyalty to themselves, but it sounds just a long-forgotten marketing gimmick out of hundred others by which you might do something on your market share, for s short period of time. If there are still categories of consumer labeled as innovator, follower and so on, nowadays I will not be surprised at a conclusion out of a consumer research that at least 30% of total consumers can be claimed as innovator in their spending patterns. Telecom market would be an appropriate example to illustrate that early entry does not at all guarantee a long lasting leading position and a success in the early years can only be sustained if you are sensitive and sensible to every market movement out there.

In general, consumers' preferences on product features and their behavior patterns are ever changing at a pace which many marketers find it difficult to follow. Some marketers are proactive enough to try manipulating the demand with their continuous introduction of new products and upgraded models. Some of them will be well received by the market but many of them prove to be a shoot in the dark. Product life cycles are becoming shorter and shorter and so are the histories of some once very good performing companies. A rush decision on a new product would easily impair your company's share in the market and instantly have your warehouses filled with obsolete stock. Maybe the decision itself is not that awful and it is simply that the appetite of the people out there 'suddenly' drops to unbearable level.

It is no exception in Chinese market. Worse enough, there are some obstacles in the way of your endeavor to understand this vast market.

Firstly, an absence of reliable data source would leave you ambiguous feelings if and how you should access your target market. In-house research would never have you cover a province the size of your home country and neither would you out-source some good quality second-hand market information. Though some international research houses do have market presence here, it would be yet a dream if they can present to you some well-structured market data for some cities other than that of Beijing, Shanghai and Guangzhou. Bits and pieces of information, outdated or not, will scatter around your team and the only good news is no matter what decision you are going to make, you can always have one piece of these information somewhere to rationalize this particular decision.

Secondly, the size of the population is so big that most the times it is a remote chance for you or any other research professional to consolidate their shopping habits or consumption behaviors into patterns of any kind. If you would be satisfied with some common conclusions like '80% of the consumers are value-for-money-minded or so' or '70% of the consumers perceive imported brands with higher quality', you need not have to finish your reading since you can also write yourself three pages of findings of the likes in twenty minutes.

Thirdly, Chinese consumers have been kept out from the western worlds and its products and services for so many years, their boredom with their existing few choices and their eagerness to try new products and services would be so strong that these Chinese consumers are ready to hop from one brand to another within months if they think it is affordable. If on average one person would spend two months to try two different brands of toothpaste product, a Chinese would have spent 4 weeks to complete the task inasmuch as he may be simply driven by his own desire, the in-store promotion, the on-pack premium or so. The variables of influential factors on their behaviors would reduce the trustworthiness of your research result to certain extent.

Also, studies on behavior patterns disclose valuable information for marketers to design the best approach to get in touch with their customers. Though it seems to me that there are seldom apparent patterns on behaviors of Chinese consumer that could be observed precisely, at least not some patterns which are indicative of a direction for the marketers to access quick success.

You might be able to observe some kind of behavior patterns in one city and stunningly detect a totally contradictory patterns the next city. Unless you are well equipped with resources for an in-depth study on all these geographical markets one by one, you would realize trying to find some common behavior patterns out of the majority of Chinese consumers is a waste of time and effort and the price would be high if you presume one successful execution of in-store promotion in Beijing will grant you another success in Shanghai.

### Self-contained economy

China has been a self-contained economy for a long time and it had somehow fulfilled its domestic demand at large scale. From daily necessities to heavy industries, Chinese people have been living on their own. Such economic system is distinguishable from the free trade economies in the west.

It has long been a tradition for the mass Chinese consumer to be offered few choices on merchandises and they succeed in making it out of a habit of using local branded goods in their daily life, without complaints on its sometimes-substandard quality, plain-looking packaging, and odd branding.

So far a large portion of the population in the age of mid thirty or above had actually grown up in one of the toughest times of this country in its modern history. They have been trained to accept, reluctantly or not this kind of life attitudes and styles. You can find them everywhere in the society, the civil servants in public administrations, white-collar class in the office, the blue-collar in the factories, the teachers in schools, the housewives at home, etc. most importantly, the fact that they are always the decision maker, the purchaser and the user of your products and services has an undeniable impact on your business future.

Believing it or not, when there are many youthful consumers are rushing in to get hold of your innovative products offering them a fantasy of nice brand name, astonishing packaging, supreme quality, there are still two groups of people in majority of the market who either resist your temptation as hard as they can by a belief of that they can live without it; or they simply pick the cheapest ones, and most likely the local branded ones, not caring of its quality, packaging or so.

They are the critical mass in the market which makes a difference in your running business at present. Unless you are patient enough with a strong financial backup for 10 years of red figures until their second generation are going to succeed this vast market decades later and behave in the way of a more westernized fashion as a consumer then.

## Who competes with whom?

Here it is apparent that there are demands across the territory on all kinds of goods and services and the demand keeps emerging here and there. The challenge is who is going to fulfill them and how. The answers to these two questions are either simple or complicated. And I am afraid I do not have a straight answer to each of them.

However, I would like to point out that many foreign investors, manufacturers in heavy industries, consumable products marketers, professional service providers and so forth, appear sharing a general misunderstanding in China that imported brands or foreign investors can easily squeeze in the market for a toehold, and effortlessly beat the local competition in no time. And therefore they are always keeping an eagle eye on their competition which they meet all the time in the global market since these frequent encounters in the other part of this planet are their real rivalries. In fact, many of them are just mistaking their rivalries; and their allies as well.

Today it is prevailing that lots of marketing principles and theories are in need of refining and re-defining when you see the blurs on more and more once-clear definitions in various areas and the lines of distinction between them are crossed over. Who would argue that the marketing strategies on durable goods like automobiles would distinctly differentiate from that of the personal computer manufacturers? Or the tactics of on-the-spot promotion for a refrigerator would significantly distinguish from that for a mobile phone? Or the routine service targeted on mass market by a bank does not require also a high level of personalization on tailor-made services like airline companies? As time goes by, you have seen the automobile manufacturers launch face-lifted models every year supported with lots of marketing gimmicks like lucky draws, TV commercials, sponsorship and etc.; you also read the leaflets laid to your place by your bank to promote their privileges banking services only VIPs are entitled to...

At the end of the day, there is probably only one definition left applicable in your business upon which all your efforts on strategy formulation, plan execution, cost budgeting, staffing and all the allocations of resources will be constructed: the difference between personal consumer or institutional customers and their respective characteristics. Customer satisfaction is the calling card.

There is no longer high-end market versus low-end market in the same product categories since one who specializes only in either segment will end up eliminated by the market when its competition succeeds in expanding his product range into both ends. And the one who specializes in high-end range and is proud of his long leading position there will soon be defeated when his competition active in low-end market seizes his share finally by launching new premium ranges. There are so many examples in the real business world you can illustrate, in the industries of automobile, telecom, food and beverages, hi-tech and computers and etc. for someone to understand there is not only vertical integration or horizontal acquisition, but also a diagonal expansion into various market segment. All these big moves by a company serve one sole purpose: to survive and to survive better.

If the above mentioned prevails, I would tend to believe if a foreign investor in a state of obsession of that he is far superior to the local companies and their brands and products, and irrationally believes that the key to his success is to defeat another foreigner, his future will be a dead-end like many investors from overseas in China at the moment.

An over-statement on the importance of market segmentation in China would turn out restraining your flexibility in adjusting yourself to responding to the market needs effectively.

China is not yet a marketplace where you can 'ascertain' its consumer demands freely by creative and powerful marketing measures. Either, you do not know a clue about where specific demands are exactly due to a lack of reliable market information for each primary affluent region you are advised.

Your positioning strategies on your brand, product and company in the first few years will be critical to your future survival. The rule of thumb would be to squeeze in the mass market and attain a firm toe-hold among some top local brands before you plot more specific medium-term strategies to beat the other imported opponents for new emerging markets. A solid presence on the mass market in the early years will empower your company and your products to earn your deserved share of market as early as possible, which in return enhance your competitiveness in the market year by year and free you from possible pressures of interferences from headquarters and weakening financial position.

To conclude, a sharing of clear definition of your short-term competitions and long-term ones among the management team will undoubtedly exert overwhelming influences on what strategies are employed to position yourself and how your resources are laid. An absence of clear understanding on the delicate interrelation between locally bred competitors and local consumers would lead to your hardworking of years and resources of millions in vain.

# Competition is fierce

Not surprisingly, China is no longer an unexploited consumer market where you can feed them with everything labeled with a sticker of 'Imported' as it was or so you thought a decade ago. Monthly business review reported from your Chinese division or 'China desk' always arrive at your office with kind of comprehensive and narrative descriptions on how fierce the competition is in China and how serious it has caused it to lag behind the plan, coupled with a devastating outlook on next month's forecast. You just wish you would get used to bad news like this very soon but you know you could not.

Is the competition in China as intense and fierce as that you personally experienced in other regions or countries where new brands and new products come and go every month, money-burning promotional campaigns are seen on the spot everywhere, enormous throat-cutting price wars are initiated on retail level? I personally do not think it could have evolved into a 'bloodthirsty' stage where some of the major markets in other developed countries have reached.

A walk in the shopping malls in the prime commercial areas in big cities like Shanghai or Guangzhou would let you have a feel on the amazing evolution of Chinese market. Local consumers are anxious to spending their disposable income on various merchandises on shelves to improve their quality of living, and the vigorous market sentiment reflects the growing market potential in the eyes of businessmen. Though in the meantime new brands and products are constantly launched and listed on shelves day after day, foreign companies keep forming their joint ventures and start their direct businesses, cost of TV commercials on prime time slot keeps setting record high year after year. You also keep yourself updated of market news about which companies are having a hard time in money collection and too high stock level, and particular brands are disappearing from the outlets, or one of your competition is going to carry out a laid-off plan to lower operating cost, etc. Based on your own recollection of what you can observe in the Chinese market, you tend to believe that marketing is indeed expanding at high pace but the competition is getting intense, it is like what are described by your management team of Chinese business. However, when the market is expanding itself and offering more and more business opportunities to the foreign investment, you might need to take a closer look at whether the competition of nowadays in China would be different in nature to that you are probably facing in other countries and market.

## Whom are you competing with?

The competition is different in a sense that you might have more than just competing with other players who are delivering the same products and services to the same population of consumers. And business nature of your investment directly affects which kind of competition you are probably facing. An investor involving in the retail sector is supposed to compete with other retailers for shoppers in the mass, prime shop locations in major commercial areas, stronger support from suppliers of merchandise and so forth; while another in manufacturing sector would be fighting against their competition for a more eye-catching shelf space in the outlets, a prime air time for TV commercials, a top-notch distributor in particular region, other than their most valuable endearing yet savvy consumers. You can imagine each story would vary slightly even though all of them are related to a matter of life or death.

As mentioned in previously chapters, a misidentification of your primary competition would expose yourself to assault from your back out of your surprise. And a causal evaluation on your competitiveness in each area will add to your vulnerability.

In China, people in various areas tend to believe there is a transparent borderline between the arenas of local companies and foreign investment and they appear more willing to prepare a heads-on competition with someone from the same side of the border though they may keep talking all the time about the possible threats posed by the groups of other side on so many occasions in the public, as you can read in many business journals or magazines in which 'east meets west' is very often a topic of common interest.

## Go for defense or offense?

Competition exists everywhere and one must face it. You are welcomed to the world and play the game of offense and defense. As long as you stay in the battlefield, you need to deal with your competition with either one as the framework of your strategy formulation at different stages of your business development.

Many foreign investors understand very well a plain fact that particular stages of your business development require them to install a combination of offensive strategies and aggressive mindset into their frontline organization and their 'think tank' inside the company to outcompete the competition while in certain phases of another scenario, a defensive approach coupled with well earned market sense on the alert will help overcome any threat posed by their rivalries.

Which approach is to be used can be largely dependent on the following: your corporate goals and objectives, your company's specific needs in particular time frame, your competitive environment and the overall market situation and its trend.

Mission statement is viewed as the ultimate goal or a description of a state of business Utopia for a company and its organization to aim at and work for. In many large corporations, it is also the most frequently mentioned in every big event like annual conferences, business review meeting. Yet it is ironically the most easily forgotten by the majority of the entire organization, let alone the annual goals and objectives laid down for your specific Chinese operation in the beginning of the commencement.

The following will ring a bell in your mind since they may sound very familiar to your own personal experiences.

In China you start with a 10-year business plan committing the operation to a break-even in the operating profit and loss by the fifth operational year and an annual growth at 25% or higher afterwards; a leading position in the market with a share of 30% or more in your product categories by the same time; launch of new product range by the fourth year to double your total net sales within two years; or merger with another joint venture company in sixth operational year for an extension to lower end market; and so forth. All these sound reasonable to the management since they are the valuable conclusions and decisions taken by a bunch of own professionals and hired consultants who have spent six months working night and day to assess all the risks and come up with such a thought-thorough plan. Anyway, the plan must be good since they are paid for the deliveries of these great jobs.

Unfortunately, it happens to many ambitious foreign investors here that the once very reasonable plan will have to be thrown away immediately after the first or second financial year are audited and reported. The magnitude of the ratio figures of actual versus plan for the first two years would just have the power to drive the readers crazy by a glance at them. Not later than the third year of operation, the heat is on from the headquarters and therefore the primary and sole objective would have to switch for you and your local management team to realize by all means a reduction of accounts receivables by 50% end of the year, and lowering the inventory level by 45% to release some more capital to keep your company survive for three months more…and the intensive pressures are already driving your staff crazy before some of them can faintly regain their composure from the record breaking low sales of last month…

When things develop like this, resources are running out and risks keep crawling around, your people, if not only yourself, are paralyzed at the wreckages and probably have failed to keep a clear mind for a proactive strategy formulation to control the damage already, when it is overwhelmingly needed most.

Seldom could you and your team remain sensitive and responsive to the dynamics of market movement, as you are already exhausted at the internal problems. Whether and how to defend or offend in the market turns out to be the last and least question in your mind as they do not bring in instant impact on your situation.

Here short-term interests override the long-term objectives even they are contradictory to each other and consequently inadequate defense or offense measures would be taken to worsen the situation without your knowing it. Sometimes a sudden U-turn shift from offense to defense will fail to serve its deemed purpose but create confusion and misunderstanding among your team. A transparent and well-organized communication system is the key for you and your staff to team up cohesively and work things out to the same direction and it evidently is not in its place.

Crisis management is an art in business and it is more than just useful for you to sustain your control on damage done to your China business. Similarly, some special project management skills like project planning, risk assessment, handling of information, and outcome evaluation and etc. can well accommodate your needs to make individuals in your company be flexible and responsive enough to the crisis and the changes that are required to tackle the crisis ahead. Most importantly, communication is the key to keep your organization attached to the core corporate strategy of defense or offense respectively.

All in all, there must not be an all-weather formula when and how a defense or offense approach would be plotted since it is strictly subject to your objectives and your specific needs. Nothing would warrant you an infinite success. Though I tend to believe that a creativity in your open mind coupled with meticulous risk assessment can better suit your in the market environment in China and place your company in a better position to compete at full force.

## *Invisible competition*

As discussed earlier, it is a conventional phenomenon that foreign investments always watch closely their other fellow competitors from overseas, even though they might not admit such a way of thinking. Ironically the Chinese businessmen share their viewpoint on this and they themselves are used to look over their shoulders at their local competitors most the times.

The Chinese market is divided into two arenas where local marketers are competing with themselves while most foreign investments in form of joint venture establishment or wholly owned enterprise are expecting heads-on encounter with their well-acquainted competition. Of course they are also some bold and ambitious players crossing the invisible border and seizing any opportunities for a niche market. However, it is more or less an opportunity-taking activity as the majority of their resources are still diverted into their primary market.

It is only until the prevailing discussion about China's accession to WTO that local enterprises appear to gradually realize the unavoidable heads-on encounter with the foreigners after protection from the government will fade away, and acknowledge the fact that they are in need of higher competitiveness against them no matter what background they might have. Though it is known to them that the sooner the better, many of them do not even know what to do and where to start. Apparently there will be heavy casualties in the first few years after China's accession to WTO granted officially.

Provided that the above will be at least part of the truth, does it mean that such change is absolutely in favor of foreign investment as many existing measures and policies enforced by the Chinese government will be revoked? I am afraid the answer is not so encouraging.

For someone who has possessed some hands-on experiences in running a business in China, regardless of type of industries and field of profession he belongs, he is aware of the mounting pressures from inside the company and the market outside. Most of the foreign investments are facing the same problem: how to catch up with their business plan by consolidating the existing business and revitalizing the brands, restructuring the organization, and etc. most people are putting the blame on the keener-than-ever competition around themselves for their dragging business in the past years in China.

As far as Chinese market is concerned, the competition in fact is not so intense as many people would have believed or described, nor it is as tense as many figures from statistics or market researches would have indicated it would be. On the contrary, I would say that the market potential and consumer demands inherent in such a big country is high enough to breed much more brands and grow much more industries than most people could imagine.

I personally have serious doubts about lots of data and statistics released by the authorities or research firms since it is always a haunting question to me if they are accurate and objective enough to rely on. For instance, my experiences have proven that a very capable internationally recognized full service advertising agency operating in China can mostly likely supply with air time monitoring for only few top cities or a big research firm can only present to you some market data for no more than top ten cities. After all, they may have to face the same problems as you do everyday out there.

Comparing the intensity of competition in China and its possible causes with the western world, it is noticeable that there exist some differences in nature, which may be worthwhile a closer look.

Competition in the west tends to intensify when the market has developed into a state of saturation where consumer demands are fully ascertained and met by the existing marketers. When there are some factors in place to affect the balancing of supply and demand like new entries of marketers or deterioration of market size, all marketers in the same industry will have to wrestling with one another for a bigger share of the market. The focus is mostly on how to win the consumers or customers over someone else or you will lose in this zero-sum-like game.

Apart from the relentless wrestling with competitors to reach, com-municate and capture your end consumers or targeted customers, of course the 'war zone' typically extends into other areas where resources of particular kinds are vital to your business. For instance, as a manu-facturer in home appliance market, you are usually looking for as much shelf space as possible in hypermarket and department store so your nice products are at arm's length of your potential consumers, and the more shelf space you are offered, the less your competitors are getting; or as a trading company in the motorcycle industry, you are expectedly anxious to obtaining sole distributorship of particular brands to monopolize the market. They are just a few of thousands of examples to demonstrate that a competition among your and your rivalries is not only in the challenge of fulfilling market demand, but also in the con-test of acquiring external resources, partnering with affiliates and sup-plier, and all the others that you are in need of such supplement to carry on in the entire flow of products and services from your company down to the market.

Nevertheless, most competitors in the west understand well that the focal challenge is laid ahead regarding how to triumph the patronages from your customers and consumers while the external resources rela-tively speaking, are openly accessible and its supplies are self-adjustable, thanks for the mechanism of capitalism.

The picture looks rather differently in China. In addition to the main challenge from your competitiveness in winning your customers or consumers, you are supposed to snatch from time to time bits and pieces of external resources along the supply chain endlessly before you may finally attain to your market. To sustain your success will be the next round of wrestling with your opponents.

External resources are much more scarce than one might have expe-rienced in the western business world. Here the external resources mean qualified wholesale channel in local distribution network to pen-etrate your products effectively, eye-catching shelf space in retail outlet and hypermarket to display your products nicely, high caliber talents in local job market to fill in your work forces, effectual mass media to communicate with your customers, reliable logistics services to deliver your products, or well managed infrastructure across the territory to support your overall operation…

Considering amounts of resources of various kinds available, and level of needs posed by huge number of marketers active in the market, the supply and demand seriously falls short of being in proportion, especially we are talking about a market in a size of a population of 13 billions in general. A bottleneck problem incurs in the middle of the transaction and it further obstructs your products and service from being well known, widely distributed, properly delivered and effectively managed.

For example, it was once a hot topic in the past few years how expensive it had been for airing your TV commercials in the prime time slots in the news report section by the state owned CCTV channel every evening. As its evening news section is a mandate for all the local TV stations in the territory to live broadcast at the same time everyday, a flash of your brands or a full shot at your products would be in theory watched by billions of potential consumers, which is clearly very tempting to some rich and ambitious marketers. As it was later handled in form of public bidding open to all advertisers of any kind, the price for a 30 seconds slot has been rising dramatically to more than 100 millions a year, meaning each minute of it would cost you hundred thousands a day and you even could not know how effective it might have reached your targeted market! When you anticipate eagerly to that there are billions of Chinese consumers nation-wide who will be watching your TV commercials everyday, you are told later a fact that there are many local TV stations that will replace the CCTV's commercials in the evening news section by their own with a help of some basic creativity in technical editing.

It is obvious that a successful foreign investor must be able to mobilize his resources in people or time or money to out-compete his rivals and reach as more consumers as possible. However, he must not downplay the importance of a competition in the areas of external resources, which are the only way to bridge up yourself with your customers. It is not necessarily a matter of if you can afford to or how much you are willing to pay for such particular resource, since on many occasions its availability is totally out of your control and there are not alternatives to choose from at all.

In some particular industries or in some geographical areas, I see that your better done jobs to access critical external resources than your competitors are even more important than your having better products or nicer brand image than your competitors. This overall environment will not change in the foreseeable future until the whole system has the inner drive to evolve into the next capitalistic phrase. Accordingly, it requires more thorough thinking and strategic business planning as far as a broader definition of competition is concerned in China.

In addition, a traditional thinking of 'competing with my usual opponents as the local brands position themselves into another arena' in China should be considered tunnel vision and narrow-minded thinking as it is getting more and more apparent that local consumers are no longer holding a naïve belief that foreign investment means better service or imported brands represent quality products. They are learning fast enough to behave like savvy consumers in the west.

## Nation-wide competition

Many foreign investors were taking the decision to enter Chinese market by the very fact that Chinese market is the most populous market in the world and its implication on business opportunities is tremendous. When your team is turned on, the dominating objectives from top management would be to establish branch sales offices in several top cities and found a distribution network of distributors on a nation-wide basis within two to three years. It is one of the very common thoughts many foreign investors are sharing on a ground that a nation-wide approach is the most cost effective and efficient to the companies itself than its alternatives, and the only way to justify the start-up capital investment in the first place. Moreover, it requires an exceptionally clear mind on analyzing the market and organizing your business when it is known to you or your boss that your peer competitors have already implemented their plan of a similar one six months ago.

Before this decision is taken, you need to ask yourselves two questions: the first would be whether you are loaded with sufficient resources on people, capital and time to carry out such a big plan nation-wide, even nationwide market coverage might have meant the top ten cities only? And the second question is whether you and your team are capable of and experienced enough to managing a 'multinational' business, in a sense of remote controlling, market adaptation, and mobility of resources.

Many investors have entrapped themselves in an irreversible situation by a too ambitious plan followed by poor execution of it and inflexibility to respond to a volatile market. A hasty decision to replicate your peers' expansion strategies in China would bear very high risks. It is like a blind leading a blind, and therefore should not be treated as a sensible alternative. A wise manager and leader should try to learn from other's successful stories and in China a wiser manager and leader would learn much more from other's failing stories.

Furthermore, a developing market full of opportunities and potentials is no longer necessarily in favor to the first comers as it was before and such favors do not last long as your predecessors might have enjoyed. A multinational company who tries to monopolize a market will find it very difficult to attain his short-lived success nowadays, as more and more variables are getting out of its control. You might spend heavily on A&P to induce buying or increase brand awareness but it just falls short of boosting up your sales or fails to strengthen top of mind recall slightly or; you might estimate your new models would have stayed in the market for the coming twelve months when all of a sudden a more powerful product invented by new technology is introduced by another company just two months later. The concept of 'life cycle' can be applicable not only to your product itself, but also your brand, your company and as a fact that a life cycle is becoming shorter and shorter; it can be both good and bad news to each of the marketers, depending their core competences to interact with the volatility of market.

The trend in international business has gradually proven that today's global market situation is more in favor to those multinational corporations and conglomerates who are typically experienced and yet creative, persistent and yet flexible, far-sighted and yet practical. Doing business in China market is no exception; especially when it is new, vastly heterogeneous, and not familiar to many global players of long histories. Not wanting to end up like some big global players who are continuously pumping money and injecting capital into their bleeding China operation like wild goose chase to fuel its titanic-like ineffective operation across the territory, you may like to caution yourself that an approach of concentration on selective geographical market would lessen your burdens all the way along your adventure into this new wonderland.

# Aggressive plans drive the business to grow in full motion

China is always associated with Confucius, who would probably be the first Chinese known to the world as his philosophies are one of the core elements in Chinese histories in the past and it is so up to now, as seen by many scholars and intellects. His philosophy of moderateness towards life has underlined the core of Chinese cultures and is still implanted into many Chinese minds nowadays. This Chinese way of thinking is still adopted by lots of Chinese businessmen today though it might not fit well in the modern business world where conservatives would more likely be defeated or eliminated.

Nonetheless, Chinese would follow their conventional wisdoms and tend to be conservative, and it is incomparable to that a foreigner would more likely learn to think big and plan bigger whenever possible.

It is not necessarily true that a foreign investor coming to China must follow the saying 'when in Roma, do as the Romans do', after all, many successes of today's multinational corporations can be attributed to their boldness in taking scarce opportunities at high risks now and then in the past. Can they repeat the same approach and have their businesses benefited in consequence of an aggressive objective setting and tough planning without their ambition overshadowed by a tower of uncertainty in the volatile market?

## *Feasibility study is not feasible*

Foreign investors who are ready to invest a great deal of money would start with a feasibility study with a view to backing their subsequent decisions with a solid and sensible ground laid down by the recommendations of the study.

First of all, most feasibility study done by professional business consultants should more or less shred a light on your basic questions on how Chinese market looks like as a whole, how much potential it is offering to the western businessmen and how the return on investment would be, and etc. However, nowadays a feasibility study to assess a business opportunity is more likely to be abused to serve the purpose of some political targets in the real world. The more it costs you, the more likely it is so, regardless of whoever is actually calling the shot, whom it was completed by, and how much it was paid for.

A feasibility study is supposed to be an activity of filtering valuable factual information and collecting usable data on the subject and based on this input, consolidating a series of objective and professional recommendation specific to the related subject by some occupational consultants or business advisors. However, if that is really the case going around us, I am afraid that our world would have not been the one we see now and the world economy would have not globalized itself as it is at present. It is because a feasibility study is always called for only after a decision is made and the study itself is proposed to answer a pointed question in an official manner with anticipated conclusions.

Someone has said that being rational makes human distinctive from other species form on earth. Doing business is also kind of human's social activities, which requires one to think the 'rational' way and make sensible decisions. Recommendations made by responsible and professional consultants in the feasibility study are the product of collective rational thinking and therefore they are to be followed respectfully whenever necessary. But there are always exceptions; their recommendations can be dropped if they are not compatible with the goals and objectives of the company or some individuals...

For instance, how can a renowned global market leader in mobile phone market tolerate its inability to claim gloriously itself in the number one position worldwide in the industry if it does not even have a toehold or modest market presence in Chinese market today, in this case not many would not be dying for a little of the whole pie at any costs. It is a matter of money and more importantly an issue of face saving. If the world market is to be divided into East and West, East resembles Asia, and China resembles the major part of Asia. Such resemblance brings in lots of fantasies and desires to many global corporations and they are convinced completely that immediate business expansion into Chinese market will be in the interests of the company and such move does fit compatibly into the ultimate goals and objectives embraced by the company and the top management indeed.

So how can one justify his burning desire and instant decision to go to China three months later? A conceivable feasibility study will do.

Consultancy industry is not charity but strictly business, therefore a good and constructive customer relationship is more than important to the firm's long-term interests if it is to stay in business. Hence, keeping the content of a feasibility study in line with its client's 'corporate needs' is not a problem at all. Thanks to your consultancy firm's understanding on these 'needs', they are sensitive enough to interpret every unspoken intention and will be honored to co-operate with his client by adequately window dressing, if not slightly doctoring, the feasibility study a little bit to offer their helping hands. Should things not be worked out as it could be, yet senior management would be prejudiced enough to downplay the value of reference of such feasibility study and turn to their own professional judgment. After all, from their viewpoint there are always some lousy consultancy firms who are making a fortune by delivering just substandard jobs.

If the study is completed by a group of in-house experts, the findings are most likely to fall exactly within the scopes of expressed views of the management since too much interference would have been stained during the process. Perhaps, it would be too harsh saying that an internal feasibility study is merely a redundancy of time and effort without which top management will anyway make the same decisions. Though, The main purposes of an request for a feasibility study are probably to evident that a decision of going China must be correct, and to clear any minor doubts and concerns in the way so most stakeholders can be relieved as much as possible.

That is why it is not surprising for me to have heard that a multinational corporation would hire more than one consultancy firm to study the feasibility of the same project sometimes. By doing so there can be recommendations and conclusions in line with individual's preferences to choose from.

There is actually another inborn fact that weakens the trustworthiness of a feasibility study for Chinese market. A responsible consultancy firm may see that any doctoring its recommendation the last thing they would do under all circumstances. However, who could guarantee the raw data or basic information collected is reliable enough, if not falsified?

In the western market, you can easily get drowned in the mountain of market data or business information that is officially published and its sources are very reliable and can be verified objectively. Your headache is merely how to extract the most referential and helpful from the massive database. On the contrary, in China you would only be accessible to some brief and out-dated and incomplete business information. Yet you could get drowned again, but in the sea of data or information which you cannot validate or verify its sources. Your headache now is not to make a judgment on which piece of information would be most helpful to your decision making, instead, you are agonized with filtering any reliable data from tons of junk information on hand.

It does matter to you and your team whether you should ever read the feasibility study; how you should interpret the findings; and what preventative measures should be in place in case recommendations are to be followed. China is picking up its pace of modernization and narrowing its distance with the western world in every aspect, but there are yet rather loose-and ill-organized sources of business information and data for any serious reference.

Considering its size and complexity, one may ready himself to the fact that gathering of accurate and complete business information or data will not be as routine as it would be in your home countries. Meticulous attention and special caution of some kind to related figures would be recommended whenever critical information or data is to be reviewed and evaluated for some once-a-lifetime vital strategic decision-making on your Chinese business.

## Sales target is mandate

A business starts with a sales plan is the most basic element in the business plan by which the management can anticipate how to allocate its resources and accordingly project the company's overall performance for each upcoming fiscal year. Sales target is directly related to a company's operating profit and loss statement and therefore, sales target and achievement of such corporate target are often the top concern of senior management, especially when profitability cannot be a very indicative to an infant business's performance and growth potential.

Many large multinational companies had been very positive and optimistic when they first were attracted to overwhelming business opportunities presented by Chinese government and started with them a relatively aggressive business expansion plan for this market. These plans might have been worked out with scant attention to its potential risks and uncertainties since Chinese market to them looked like just a 'black hole' where it can take in everything and the people there are willing to buy whatever you are presenting to them on shelves. It is a 'black hole', in a sense it sucks in your resources too.

In many cases it is because an aggressive plan with a growth rate of 40 or 50% each year that many foreign investors have ended up with running out of resources, falling short of sales target, piling up of obsolete stock, and suffering from heavy accounts receivable. And the consequence of a too ambitious sales plan is very often an over-estimation on the manageability of the Chinese market coupled with a scant evaluation of its risks. It is deadly wrong if one would presume a big market like China could allow you to make some mistakes then, you can yet reverse it at an affordable price!

For those who have already been paralyzed by repetitive failures at achieving the annual plan benchmarked by its 10 years business plan specified in your first feasibility study, it would be wise to just put aside of that 'blue sky' plan and review the total business situation again. By doing so, you may again found a new business plan from your own experiences gained.

Relentless learning is the word of wisdom in such a volatile market like China. A learning organization is the most valuable asset for your company to edge out your competition one day. Anyhow you have paid the 'admission fee', no matter how expensive it had been; therefore your hands-on experiences will encompass you to the right direction.

If you are convinced that your business unit in China cannot be managed by your usual and conventional ways of management system as many of your other subsidiaries aboard are; for the reasons of its unique market characteristics or the fact that the situation is close to a calamity at the moment, a patch of remedial measures in exercise will be far from enough to rescue your business from falling. As a matter of fact, many companies have been exhausted patching by bits and pieces of so-called remedial measures to fix their problems and fails to spare any resources to cope with any new market changes already. Unless you and your team have the courage and determination to radically apply a dose of 'strong medicine' to cure your existing sick business, your only way out might have been a retreat from the market until you are ready again, as some once-popular brands and companies had chosen to.

As said before, your late arrival may not necessarily put you in an inferior position where it hinders you from out-competing your peers and taking over leadership one day for the years to come. There is no need to worry about being left behind in Chinese market as there can only be more and more new opportunities rising from such a booming market.

Of course a decision like this would be a nightmare and so that many of them would take alternative measures to stay in business. Nonetheless, it is advisable that if one is anxious to having his Chinese business in a better shape, they should try harder in re-engineering their Chinese operation than just window-dressing every year the end results by lowering the annual target at the last minute every year, revising the plan four times a year, suspending any necessary A&P expenditures just to better off the profit & loss situation. There have been too many average managers abusing these shortsighted and narrow-minded tricks at the expense of a brighter future of the companies and the interests of the shareholders.

## Money collection set high in agenda

China has been famous in the international business world for its notorious problem on 'triangle-debt' problems for at least couple of decades. It has been endangering so many state owned enterprises, which were finally choked to death by long-time mal-management and bureaucratic inefficiency.

When there have come more and more foreign investments participating into Chinese market, they are not blessed with their relatively experienced financial controlling expertise and gradually are entrapped as well. Since then, the name of the game is 'money collection'.

It may appear simply a common sense that a company has to remain financially sound and it can be done by installing a rigid and prudent financial controlling system in the company. As a matter of fact, many well-known global companies are quite experienced in this area and therefore they can stay at the top of the world for long time and each detail in their controlling mechanism is optimized relentlessly to protect the company to the greatest extent. They have been proud of their full knowledge and expertise in this area and of course they should, however, they would tend to turn this vital function into kind of some routine managerial activities in their Chinese business operation and this careless mistake would be downplayed to compensate the need of a loose control by any start-up infant businesses. Anyway, everything is cheap in China and therefore no spending could result in a big loss, isn't it?

Their light-heartedness in dealing with the exceptional financial risks in China would lead to unbearable risks before long, as many examples has showed the severe damages done to some multinational companies by their ballooning accounts receivables quarter after quarter.

People are getting too excited every time they are about to enter a new market and the most often question asked would be how much sales we would generate for the first five years and how much share of the total market we can tap over our competition. Most of them would suddenly be oblivious with the prime importance of a sound financial position to a new setup. A business plan for the new China division would cover every detail of what are supposed to be covered except that a concise projection of how the item of accounts receivables resulted from a demanding sales target for each year would impact on the infant business's financial soundness. Even there is such an analysis, not many people care to address the topic from the viewpoints of their profession as usual.

One who is in charge of the Chinese operation would need more sales turnover to affirm that the decision of going China is not at least a dump decision, though its profitability so far has proven it cannot be a very wise decision either. Pursuit on sales achievement by causal selling in China is likely the most convenient stimulus to bring about doubtful debts or bad debts in your Chinese business and must be very costly. You might succeed in getting some nods from the big bosses to break some financial rules and guidelines once or twice so that you can compromise a bit for the tough situations a year or two. Nevertheless, you should have known that financial people are kind of working by the rules all the time and therefore least patient to any unusual treatment by exception, especially when they are not rewarded by any positive signs after the first time they keep their eyes closed once.

When your colleagues from the financial controlling function start to lose their patience, your big bosses will too. Since there will be more and more people talking at your back and papers and reports and reviews will fly all over the desks of the power persons.

It is actually a calculated risk whether and how you will make the highest sales turnover as possible while an acceptable risk level of receivables is maintained, depending on your specific goals and objectives. Frankly speaking, in western world selling could be in general the toughest part for the company to accomplish as it is the first round of your direct contact with your market and it gives good indication whether your business can be a success or not. The general presumption is that once you sell, your customers and clients will usually pay, on whatever terms. In case you are in need of any legal advice, you are free to consult legal advisors and you feel the protection from the reliable legal system as safety net around you. Hence, a signed sales contract or the physical delivery of your products to your customer can be viewed as the milestone to pronounce the done deal. And from then on, the rest of the tasks in the transaction would be just kind of follow-up tasks to officially complete the business transaction, including money collection. That may be one of the reasons there are also some big and successful companies which have their accounting departments to contact their customers for due payment, instead of their front-line sales force who are the ones doing the selling jobs. Similarly, the treatment of western accounting principles also leave a lot of room for individual corporations to handle accounts receivables at their own discretion, so there are various tailor made guidelines applied by themselves in different companies and the application in the same group of companies may even vary slightly to fit the particular situation.

If the above mentioned is the general perception and common practices in the western world, here In China, however, the situation would be more complicated than just that.

In China, the last thing you can do to surprise a businessman is to tell him how hard a company would have tried to keep a clear slate on its money collection performance at an acceptable level. Chinese people are not well trained to evaluate and control financial risks, as far as credit control is concerned. The most impressive feature of a typical Chinese way of handling accounts receivables must be its absence of any concept of bad debt or doubtful debt. Therefore, you will never find an item called 'bad debt provision' or similar items in their financial reports, as required by the state. It is understandable that the reason why it is not allowed is for some purposes of inland revenues. Restricted by this policy, nobody can play creative accounting to doctor the figures and all the booked sales turnovers are eligible for taxation, regardless of whether you can realize its profit by collecting the money or not.

Owing to a lack of due understanding in the importance of a rigid credit control, coupled with a tunnel vision of the definition of selling tasks, many state owned companies had long suffered from severe financial problems caused by bad debts and gone bankruptcy at the end when the situation develops beyond tolerable level. Such dysfunction of the business sector has throttled a chain effect on the circles of foreign investments in China as well. Striving to higher sales turnover to beat the target and plan, many foreign investments have been working around the potential problems arisen from customer's inability to pay the bills with a high hope that they would be luckier than some peers as victims in the stories they have been told. Not surprisingly, many of them get caught off-guarded.

This mistake could have been avoidable. Senior management of a foreign investment should keep an eagle eye on their credit controlling mechanism for their clientele as they do in the west at least, if not more strictly. Credit analyses done by the rare third-party company search

firm for most of local Chinese business partners would be of no reference to you because the market is yet too primitive to pick up in this
area. For those reports I personally had seen, even a professional firm
could rarely come up with a report detailed enough to base some decisions on. Your financial controlling team must keep alert on the daily
transaction and have the management posted of any doubtful ones. It
can be a battle of nerves but one can always learn something when a
lesson has been taught for so many years.

Training of some kinds to educate the front-line sales force on credit
control and evaluation on customer's financial ground would be of
assistance to keep the company away from 'dangerous' customers.
Brainwash is hard, but it may work better if it is linked somehow to
your compensation scheme offered to your sales team in the very
beginning of their field days.

The last but not least, attention must be paid to the level of
accounts receivables and intensive financial analyses should be conducted from the management whenever the business is reviewed, other
than its performance on sales achievement and profitability. It is
beyond doubt that achievement on sales target and profit target respectively are good indicators to show if the company is on the right track
at the right pace, however, such bias would be misleading your operating management team to maneuver too much of their effort on these
two elements and consequently overlook the ageing reports signaling
concerns of particular customers on particular transactions. Without a
routine but unbending credit control policies over your sales activities
in China, a foreign investor will probably further suffer from a cycling
effect on its overdue debts soaring, ageing of accounts receivables worsening, sales turnover plunging, inventory level building up, cash flow
thinning, and etc. The joint influence of all these dysfunction would
lead to an irreversible state where the management is just too panicking
to arrive at some sensible decisions to turn around the situation.

Only a sharpened understanding of the fatal importance of credit
control among your people, in addition to an in-time corrective mea-

sures in place and a regular review by top management on this subject would give your Chinese business an armor from horrible financial chaos and increase your chances to run a financially solid business with a future.

# Patience and persistence are the master keys to win

Having market presence for years in China, many foreign investments and its joint venture companies are still faced with a stagnant business situation in the market and in search of an exit from the blind alley.

Though yearly performance of the business has fallen short of plan for consecutive years and capital injection fails to revitalize the operations, some good managers do have the vision and sense to predict the tough times through which their businesses will have to survive before they can relieve themselves from big surprises and embarrassment in the annual reports. They are really learning from their own or their peers' precious mistakes and are voluntarily to start their business in China on a lower starting point and expect not unhappily deficit in the profit and loss statement for the first few years. Their extraordinary patience is supposed to earn them tremendous rewards in return in a wider frame of time to compensate what they might have paid. Sometimes this approach of kind of conservation would work, but in many other times it just would prolong your pain in a lesser degree for a longer time, and anyway the outcome would just happen to be the same, a solo walk in the dark and whistling still.

## Patience buys you time

Patience is a quality from which the future of your business would be benefited only when there is no viable alternative in sight for you, as it enables you to buy time till you and your team are ready at full force. A responsible manager cannot rely on it with a high hope that the adverse situation would vanish unconditionally and be replaced with a handful of golden times ahead all of a sudden. A volatile market like China does not allow someone with a 'wait-and-see' attitude to reap worry-free success without sweating effort. Your peers keep pouring their resources to solidify their foothold and build up their bridgehead, new technologies keep emerging to eliminate the weaker and its owner, and the customers are tempted to switch among brands and suppliers.

A properly devised business plan for your Chinese business does not resemble a plan composed with a conservative thinking. A good business plan for your new operation should be aggressive enough to drive your people to dedicate into the tough tasks and show their persistence into the sustainable success through their continuous effort. It is always the case that your new investment into Chinese market bring in only deficits, or at least no profit, into your existing group profit and loss, top management should not take for granted for the fact that your earnings from well established markets can and ought to finance this operation unconditionally. Recent failures to achieve the plan in the early years have usually discouraged the management from paying enough attention to their Chinese business, either because its impact on their overall performance is minimal or because they have just simply lost the impulsive interest on this market and try to sweep it under the carpet. Instead of being proactive to the situation, the management team would pretend oblivious to the necessity of serious business review and re-formation of strategy and start 'playing ostrich' by putting their heads in the sand. From now on, the name of the game is 'patience'.

However, most the times patience is a luxurious hobby in the business world since it always requires your company to have a deep pocket. Constraints and restrictions in penetrating into this Chinese market may be somehow exaggerated subconsciously in the reports and in various meetings so that some persons responsible for the outcome would rationalize their handicap in working on the problems.

These people have to pray everyday that there comes no good news from their peers or otherwise, they will be questioned very soon by the big bosses why they cannot just deliver what other could. Few heads might be chopped unhappily. Of course fire-and-hire is not the best approach and it sets a very inappropriate example by the top management to show their silly 'tunnel vision' to the public.

When your Chinese business is not performing, there would be a lot of reasons. It may be due to the management incapability to observe the market, organizational handicap to operate effectively and efficiently, poor reception of your product to the market, substandard performance of your promotional strategies, and etc. etc. All in all, no matter what the ultimate reasons would have been, they are not going to diminish unconditionally as time clicks. Proactive attitude and immediate action are two of the pre-requisites for you and your team to work on the problem. It is irresponsible for some senior managers in the headquarters to bear a thinking that it does not matter if their Chinese division is running at deficit for eternity since their well established market in Europe or United States have been so successful so that they have not at all any problem to finance it whenever it is necessary. This mode of thinking is really dangerous and as a matter of fact there does exist in many heads inside lots of multinational corporations, unfortunately.

If you are not serious about your every piece of business around the world, no matter whether you are having headache with it or not, it is advisable that a direct investment should be avoided. Window dressing to make a global market presence can be done various ways, by picking up either a sole distributor or a local trader. Chinese market is a market that requires serious masterminds coupled with advanced management skills and thoughtful marketing strategies or it would cost you much more than you could have imagined at the very beginning.

## *Down-to-earth feasibility study*

Not many senior management teams of multinational corporations are borne to have patience, until they are paralyzed by the bad news brought in on their business units somewhere across the oceans then they understand how patience is deadly needed to make their own lives easier.

Actually nobody would have had any idea how its business in China would go when something rings the bell and drives a senior manager to give it a serious thought of going China. Thanks to the inventor of feasibility study, with an in-depth study by professionals on the viability of a new business, it shreds a light on the unknown and empowers the senior management to make strategic decisions. However, the most deadly importance of a feasibility study is not its inherent value of reference and information, a good feasibility study is usually built in with a feature that allows people to review and evaluate the correctness of such strategic decisions.

There are some senior managers who have been so successful in steering their business for the past decades and been so experienced in fighting the toughest ever battles in their lives, that they just are overwhelmed with their own 'gut feelings' or business acumen. In these cases the feasibility studies would have become a formality and regardless of what it is written inside, they are ignored lightheartedly, if not their contents are somehow bent to fit into the already made decisions.

Though as said before, Chinese market is yet too lacking in reliable information and data to help the professionals to analyze it by scientific management expertise and come up with an insightful and indicative feasibility study, its findings should not be doctored in sole purpose of supporting whatever decisions senior management would have hurried themselves to make in advance.

As far as I have seen, a hurried strategic decision by foreign investment in China always is followed by a very promising business plan that every figure is very eye-popping and mouth-watering in the paper, and the figures stay only in this strategic paper for years.

Business opportunity is the twin brother of momentum, and it would be nice for a businessman to identify the momentum and grasp the opportunity to grow his business. Nevertheless, momentum is not once-a-life-time nor is an opportunity. To put it in a very simple perspective for the sake of argumentation: if your personal experiences would have told you that a golden business opportunity would on average emerge every a year in the market of your interest, I would tend to believe there will be one every three months in China. It should be the last worry that you should bother yourself on the scarcity of opportunity in a fast developing market in China.

It is admitted that the potential in Chinese market is enormous and the demand keeps growing at high rate in many industries. In general it will very soon be the biggest market for almost each kind of businesses and industries for it accommodates the biggest population in the world. This fact alone could explain why business opportunities are emerging more intensively and frequently than ever elsewhere for the coming years.

Because of this, it may not be wise to emotionally hurry a decision and rush unprepared into this market since there are always upcoming opportunities in the foreseeable future when you and your team get ready. We should learn to believe in professional advices other than your legal advisors or management accountants or IT specialists and peruse your feasibility study in expansion in Chinese market without biased personal feeling or knowledge. If a down-to-earth feasibility study unveils a warning on the viability of your China project, you had better take a serious second look and convince your colleagues to do the same before a collective decision will be made.

Furthermore, a well-conducted business plan is the blueprint on which you will base all your resources and talent to baby-sit your new Chinese business, and therefore it should by all means reflect all the realities even they might not look very encouraging. You should be aware that once you have built up your business in a market and failed to grow it or at least keep it in a good shape, it might require doubled and tripled efforts and time for you to re-build it again. Re-entry into a market with a clear slate is only a dream out of reach in the business world. A success story can win a company a reputation and so can a failure, in a sense.

## *A grip on financial controlling*

Patience does cost you not only invaluable time, but also money and other resources as well. Your business is not stationary and therefore you need to spare your resources to keep the 'machine' running. Here you can realize how crucial your meticulous attention to all financial aspects of your investment in China really is, especially when your operation does not remain a very promising financial position now and in the near future.

Many foreign investment are anxious with financial figures when they first read the feasibility study of their China project and very soon they will lost interest and fail to lay their eyes on the financial reports for more than five minutes, until they are awaken by the phone calls from the top bosses twelve months later asking them to review seriously the financial soundness of the business and submit their recommendation within one week.

In my opinion, it is to me that managing an on-going business is kind of a science whereas managing a new business is totally an art. You can learn and apply various well-established management skills and tools to your existing business in order to keep it in a good shape, but you seldom are guaranteed that particular skills and methods will help you manage and grow your new business to be successful. As a result of such an unknown and unpredictable future, one is exceptionally in need of some special skills and talent to tackle the challenges laid ahead of him. However, these skills or talent may not necessarily be brand new and tailor-made for your special needs but there are many fundamental skills by which you can baby-sit your new business as effectively as you do for your well-run business elsewhere.

One of them is a rigid and prudent financial controlling practice. Financial controlling is a function area where you have your financial specialists and managers help you to monitor your business and alert you of any potential problems whenever necessary. A very close collaboration between general management and financial controlling function is the key to clear many difficulties in the way to success for a new business in China.

First of all, in China there are different set of accounting rules and principles and also a different set of financial treatment and interpretation. Many foreign investors are too concerned with their Chinese operation's ability to comply with their international accounting standards and financial reporting requirement and they prefer either their own expatriate financial expert filling in this key position, or a group of own financial advisors sent from headquarters working 'closely' with the locally hired controller. These approaches as most people would know, have its pros and cons. Understanding its advantages and disadvantages is an issue, but trying to eliminate the disadvantages is another, and the latter is far more important for the senior management from the headquarters to work on. Here the relevant expertise and harmonious working relationship are two main obstacles to overcome.

To illustrate, it is imperative that your financial controlling function has the in-depth professional knowledge and skills to handle his jobs in compliance with the Chinese way of accounting and financial treatment. The conversion of the set of accounting books and financial reports can be tackled by expert consultation with headquarters in the short term and staff training and orientation in the medium term. Besides, a cautious financial controlling practice will always give insightful conclusion to senior management whether and where risks lays in the business and therefore, it is especially vital for you and your team to keep an eagle eye on all financial implications regularly and scrutinize the reports in order to make sure your infant business is on the right track.

To do so, you need a high caliber financial expert to empower your controlling team, though the fact is many foreign investments have been more than willing to pay a king's ransom for a local sales director or even a brand manager when they offer only a very tight budget for hiring an experienced financial manager. Eventually their businesses in China turn out to be a house of card and cannot stand up to the slightest turbulence in the market. Such disasters have to be partially attributed to their loose controlling from the perspective of finance and they are caught off-guarded easily.

Whether financial controlling is more important or valuable than your sales and marketing function in your China project is a question depending your particular industries or business sectors, however, it must be clear that financial controlling is not simply a function to help you 'massage' the figures when you need it. When most general management are borne to be ill at numbers and some others are just allergic to any ratios or numbers, percentage, hunches cannot win the games all the times and your decisions may not be the best ones sometimes. In such a dynamic and unknown market like China, you may have to rely on your financial controller to best understand your on-going business and respect and review their advices whenever possible. After all, the earlier you identify any approaching risks, the sooner you can launch any precaution measures.

## Cost saving saves your business

During the times of economic downturn, we all have cost saving programs of every kind in most companies of each industry in every size to improve our businesses. There would be other fancier names like re-structuring or re-engineering, but they serve the same purpose, and it is to increase the competitiveness and productivity of your business.

When you are about to finish your cost saving program, you would find how much of your limited resources have been wasted in the past years and if they had been allocated and utilized in a more effective manner, you would have not needed to have put some additional resources on the program itself. No matter how smart your management team can be, short memories let these managers make the same mistakes over and over unless your companies are self-contained with an effective mechanism to monitor and control your spending.

Agreeing with it or not, many senior management of lots of foreign companies investing in China are making various expensive decisions which result in unnecessary spending and wastes up lots of capital investment.

To illustrate, they decide to move in the most luxurious office complex in the prime commercial areas not to build prestigious corporate image or try to impress their customers, but for their own comfort with a nice view out of the window. If they ever visit their local customers' offices, they would have realized that most of their customers' offices are far below their standards and they just cannot even have the sense or taste to feel impressed by your nice offices. It would be fine if your company would afford comfortably this luxury, though it will be rather ridiculous when there are still decade-old equipments that its ownership was transferred from your Chinese business partner to your joint venture company, laying around your production plant, or there are still workers packing your products into carton boxes by manual or so. To put it in a simple word, it is called misallocation of resources.

A responsible senior management is in a position to look after their allocation of resources everywhere in each business process and they will not rely on self-discipline of their line managers since the future of the whole company would be at stake when its productivity weakens sooner or later.

'Generous spending' in a company can be viewed as an infectious disease, which will spread over the whole organization and multiply your loss consequently easily.

Cost saving program is not a one-time campaign on ad hoc basis and should be adopted as a regular and routine policy throughout your organization. Most foreign investors who have various form of overseas investment in China would have to delegate high level of autonomy to their local management teams and expect they would exercise their authorities and rights in a very responsible fashion. In many cases it just reveals that the stories do not always unfold this way, unfortunately.

There are not many precautions to stop it from happening and it is advisable that a power financial controlling is in place to represent the best interest of the whole corporation, if you are not confident in your general manager's ability in numbers or his knowledge of basic finance. Exploring a new market like China, who would better suit the position of a general manager than someone who possesses years hands-on experiences in front-line functions like sales or marketing? They are the pioneers to lead the company into its new journey and usually loaded with key responsibilities and authorities. As a result, there are very often some kinds of conflicts between the general management and finance function as these two parties are seemingly presumed to work on an odd relationship, in many senses. You would expect some hot discussions whenever a general manager and his financial controller are convening together in the same conference room for more than 10 minutes...one insists on a price reduction to recruit more wholesalers to carry your products whereas the other one rejects any ideas which would drain away the profit margin immediately; or one stresses the necessity of a tighter credit control whereas the other one would criticize its posing a threat to sales turnover. It is a war between discipline and flexibility by tradition.

Whatever organizational structure you place your people into or however you specify the scope of authorities and responsibilities for your general management and financial controlling function respectively, financial controlling is and will be constantly a core line function for your Chinese business and therefore should not be attended only when your Chinese business is edging to a financial crisis.

China is an operating environment that you see fluctuating market demand, evolving rules and regulations, ambiguous information and rumors. All these would foster uncertainties and risks. No matter what these uncertainties and risks are and how they present themselves, they eventually have some financial implications to your Chinese operation on the spot and it is always financial problem that would strangle a business to death. It is worthwhile bearing in mind that 'casualness on performing your financial controlling would lead you to casualties'.

What would be more pathetic than that you entrap yourself with your own innocence and silliness before you even take the chance to fight a glorious fight against your competition?

## Learning organization

If your organization is not capable of learning from their own previous experiences or from the experiences of other companies in the same industries and stand up to the challenges, the more patient you are, the greater dangers your business is facing with. It is expensive for a foreign investor to be patient operating his business in China, because it will cost him a tidy sum to keep his business from disappearing in the market completely.

To illustrate, many foreign investments are most likely now in the middle of their ten-year business plan after they started their Chinese operation five years ago. Large number of them have gradually expanded their businesses into most of the coastal cities with a large organization manned with large sales team to service customers in various sizes across the nation, and the situation is even more complicated in the case of manufacturers who have various production plants to run. One can easily imagine how costly it has to be for them to keep the business running, not to mention the extra effort and time if improvements are to be made.

A foreign investor is patient but not yet able to learn and improve their own will be ill fated and before long its resources will drain away sooner than his patience does. An organization refusing to learn is eventually invulnerable to the ever-changing market environment. Your success of today in the west will not be translated into a success in the east if it is thought of as just another business expansion that you had gone through entering one of the western countries years before.

# Localization contributes to a healthier business

Business expansion into overseas always comes along with outbound organization and therefore require you to remotely mastermind your overseas business and manage the local organization by some effective means.

A company that grows successfully in its domestic market with good products and services will sooner or later consider its future role in a larger market, voluntarily or not. Such consideration could usually have been a consequence of drive from external environment, though there are also some cases the strategic decision is necessitated by a consensus ambition of the top management to walk across the threshold of world market. Most the time top management of a company is driven to go abroad by the higher interest of the company's shareholders, forces from domestic competition, stagnant demand of domestic market, and so forth. Regardless of whatever the reasons behind such discretion, the phenomenon would be that not many corporations have been well prepared for this strategic move as they think they are. Before long they would meet with unexpected problems and uncalculated risks all the way along their adventure to the new marketplace. Some of them would simply disappear from the global stage after their resources nearly dry out, some other would be lucky enough to keep walking on the thin line for years with still a high hope of future success not far away ahead.

The most demanding challenge out of all is how to adapt your corporation including its products and services, its organization, its management systems, its policies and procedures, its norms and cultures into the newly invested market in a way it would not obstruct the growing of your business but on the contrary, help enhancing your productivity of the overall Chinese operation.

Localization would be the answer, considering people would be the ultimate factor from which most of the other elements in a business could originate. A good organization would help you create and source and establish the best 'hardware' available in your Chinese operation, here hardware would in a very broad meaning, be everything you need to materialize your China project. 'People' in your organization are the sole 'software' to breathe life into your company and your 'hardware'. Without it your China project is of uselessness even you now have the best tailor-made plans, strategies, and systems for your China market in your hands.

## *People the most valuable asset*

Many global corporations are used to convey a message to their employee, domestic or overseas, all over the world that they care about people and value them the most precious asset in the company. On each social occasion, in corporate anniversary banquet, departmental regional conference or so, 'people as the most valuable asset to the company' is repeatedly mentioned in the speeches of the big bosses and they even set up internal communications divisions in the headquarters to mainly promote this motto with corporate newsletters and circulations.

Though I personally observe this phenomenon from my experiences in these kind of activities and have found that most of the speakers who mentioned this motto or similar are not the biggest boss in the companies and I start to doubt if they are representing the companies saying this or, actually they are merely taking these opportunities talking to their own supervisors or superiors about themselves…

It is much easier saying than doing for a company in this regard, especially a global corporation which comprises of people of different ethnics, culture, values, background and etc. In these days the belief of 'people as an asset to the company' would be fading away when there are more and more business processes getting workerless and automated with the helps of high technologies. Perhaps some global companies who hire tens of thousands of employees would think of a burden instead of an asset as their employees are now making more troubles than the computer-controlled machineries or assembly lines.

This assertion may have been or will be abandoned in the business world, but it is yet very appreciated by the general public of Chinese people in the workplace. The typical Chinese way of business management always involves personal relationship and Chinese employees are therefore more emotionally attached to their superiors and the companies than the westerners do. It is notable that many Chinese employees would be used to a more 'humane' organization or management style in the workplace. On the contrary, they tend to perceive foreign investors from the west as purely employers and their relationship with the foreign employers would be just an employer-employee link specified in the employment contract.

People would be the most valuable asset here in China to an organization and the company. If the management of a company would succeed in aligning the Chinese employee's emotional attachment to the company by proper motivations, their performance in their works would be stunningly excellent. A sense of belonging to the employer or the management would unite them together and drive them to the common goals.

To achieve this requires different kinds of motivation to build up a close relationship between the management and the general employees. Figure head and role model in the management team can help the whole team to exercise effective leadership in the whole company and cultivate a harmonious ambiance in the workplace to facilitate the daily operations, after all, Chinese people are still used to adore a leader in the long histories and they would loyally follow their leader once they are convinced he has earned their respects.

To sum up, managing Chinese people in the workplace is one of toughest parts as they are composed of individuals with different backgrounds, mentality, culture, values and habits, even on the junior level. It is like in your affiliated companies in United States where you have a group of people coming from different countries working together. You had better learn by the fact that Chinese people love to mention which province they are from when they introduce themselves to others. A thoughtful consideration of this fact would be helpful for a foreign investor to deal with his Chinese employees when policies on human resources are deployed.

## Expatriate is worth their handsome pay?

It is unavoidable for many foreign investors to import professionals and experts from overseas into China when they start up their business in this country without thorough knowledge of whether and where needed talents are available.

When there have been more and more foreign investments coming to China for the past decades, the local job market is gradually developing rapidly with a supply of younger generations of talents for the foreign investments nowadays. However, it seems not the stimulus to the fact that more and more foreign investors are localizing their organization, especially the middle management level, instead, it is more likely because cost saving is calling the shot when the companies are suffering from low productivity and ineffectiveness. As a result, instead of formerly filling their mid-level management positions with staff from other Asian regions like Singapore, Hong Kong and so on, the trend is now replacing mid-level management with Mainland Chinese.

Regardless of whether the new business is ready for such kind of restructuring, localization in many foreign investments is somehow accelerated by an internal need of cost saving when it is well known that expatriates are always expensive to keep. It would be a dangerous move, however.

Given the aforesaid management problems mentioned in earlier chapters, a rush into the process of localizing the mid-level managerial grades may lead to a vertical communication breakdown very soon in the organization. Obviously there have been many high caliber Mainland Chinese young managers who have great potential for further development in some top cities in Shanghai, Beijing and Guangzhou, where the elites from all other provinces are flowing in. However, there are more pre-requisites for a manager to take up more responsibilities in a foreign-invested company than simply good command of English.

Many global corporations seemingly arrive at a conclusion that a Chinese manager who can communicate with the management in English or their mother tongues would highly probably understand their requirements better and therefore can deliver the jobs in better quality. Consequently, they excessively rate too much the importance of the 'language' factor as far as recruitment of Chinese staff is concerned, and sometimes omit the importance of other basic but crucial pre-requisites that a capable staff should possess. These pre-requisites include relevant working experiences, business acumen, sense of responsibility, willingness to learn, self-discipline, exposure to western management system and etc.

I have met many Mainland Chinese managers who can speak fluent English and communicate effortlessly well with other expatriate managers, though they are not quite equal at their jobs due to various reasons like a lack of relevant experiences, unwillingness to learn, improper working attitudes and etc. Yet it appears to me that they have great potentials to grow themselves to good managers, however, taking responsibilities disproportional to their capabilities too early is doing harm to their personal growth as well as the future of the company in the long run. For instance, it is notable that in many affiliated companies of multinational corporations in China you can find their human resources managers were formerly working in office administration function in another company, or the brand manager was previously a secretary in another company and later they are offered the chances to serve their existing employers in a totally different capacities. I personally do not believe that this kind of switching between fields of business could be common in other countries. And the main reason for this is that many foreign employers are too easily impressed by their command of English in the interviews while they are in the meantime too dying for English-speaking employees to fill in their openings.

I strongly believe that language is merely a medium to facilitate the jobs and a job can never be done better simply because the incumbent can speak fluent English and not because he has the professional knowledge and relevant experiences in relation to their responsibilities. It may be reasonable that a company may hire an employee and let him learn some foreign language later so he can better perform his functions, but it will be a big mistake if a company assume a staff who can read well what is written in English in his job descriptions will naturally know exactly how to finish those jobs.

There are no standard rules in association with when and how you should localize your organization in China nor there is any in the west. Expatriate staff is expensive but they may be worthwhile your investing on them. Many of them deserve the handsome compensation from you if they are expected to help you develop and train up your local team in a period of time, say two to three years. A common mistake for many foreign investments in China is that they neglect the importance of their roles in 'coaching your local team' whose members are supposed to succeed the management responsibilities of the local business in the long range. When they are to get rid of these expatriates to lower the overhead costs in the bleeding Chinese business, there is nobody experienced and trustworthy enough to carry on the business. And many of them have ended up in a dilemma eventually.

Considering the benefits of expatriate managers on training up for you a succeeding local team, I personally do not think they are expensive in general. Localization or not depends on whether you have the right succeeding team ably ready to take over and should not be judged strictly from the perspective of financial implications.

## General 'messenger' and 'many-drink' director

To foreign investments, expanding their business into Chinese market is definitely a strategic business decision. This strategic move requires various departments and parties inside the whole organization to mobilize themselves to meet this change. The most logical explanation for their determination would be that they are convinced by the great market potential in Chinese market and therefore are willing to divert their resources into this and hopefully reap a success in their prosperous future. It is a matter of re-allocation of resources, to say the least.

Other than the constant funding for the new establishment in China, they invest a lot in the people in the new organization as it is well-known fact with the right people, they would make things happen. At least it is said so.

It is understandable that in China, expatriate executives and managers hold most of the top management positions in the joint venture companies of these global corporations. Many expatriates are actually seconded by the headquarters from one of another subsidiaries and they are picked because they have a proven track record in the companies, they are experienced executives and managers, and they supposedly can build up a new business from scratch to the satisfaction of the board of directors in the headquarters. However, how many expatriate executives and managers in China are delivering their jobs with which the big bosses are satisfied so far? I am afraid the answer would be a bit scary as long as you learn how many investments from these famous global players in China are still running at a loss, or how many years they have been fallen short of plan so far, or how frequent the top management positions are changing hands in many joint venture companies in China every year!

Many people just cannot help asking the question why it would happen this way. Surely there must be some reasons behind.

I tend to agree that many multinational corporations are picking the wrong persons to manage their investments in the first place. From what we can observe, an expatriate's proven track record in the similar capacity in other market is not necessarily a guarantee for another successful story in China, especially those who are too mentally tied with the convention and rules of western business world to initiate any self-adjustment. You will be astonished at finding out how many expatriate executives who are now working in China have never been Asian region before, not even once. They might be talented with excellent business acumen, possess professional knowledge and intensive experiences, but they are totally unfamiliar with the market itself. If you think it is just fine to understand a market by some figures in the market research data or business magazines for an expatriate, it is not the case for Chinese market. Your understanding on the Guangdong market may not be applicable to Greater Shanghai region in terms of consumer behavior, competition, or business environment. Accordingly, they will fail to acquire basic understanding on this big and heterogeneous market quickly enough and in the meantime, they inevitably need to hurry spontaneously a lot of strategic decisions, which will have deadly long-term impact on his capacity to do the jobs in the future.

In addition, there are actually many multinational corporations that are sending only average people to China since their existing businesses elsewhere do not allow them to re-locate their top-notch executives and managers into China or as a matter of fact, an assignment to working in a developing country like China is never really a very attractive offer at all to them. The alternative would then be for you to look for someone in the job market, though it is also a very risky decision since there are actually not many qualified executives and managers for Chinese market and there are much fewer available for hire.

A shortage of high caliber executives and managers internally and externally leads to the fact that there are not a small number of average people now filling up many high-ranking positions in foreign investments in China and at the same time ballooning the overhead costs of the operating business.

You will see there are some so-called general managers of a joint venture companies whose weekly work schedule are likely to include the following prioritized items:

1. Collect weekly report from individual department heads (as he needs to summarize them into his own version of weekly business overview and send it over to the headquarters every Monday);

2. Chair the inter-departmental meeting every Thursday (as he needs the minutes to keep his secretary busy for two days);

3. Learn mandarin every Tuesday and Friday evening;

Also, some expatriates are spending their time more eagerly in the pubs and bars and they would be most clear-minded in the first five minutes in the pub every Friday evening for the whole working week. What they do in their daily schedule is mainly to pay courteous visits to their customers every month and get drunk in the countless banquets and parties.

Definitely there are still respectable expatriates who endeavor to grow their companies and strive to fulfill the plan of every year to the best interests of the corporations. It is only that many more average ones are taking advantage of the fact that so many multinational corporations are so anxious to entering into Chinese market and sometimes underestimate the possible damage to their overall China project should wrong decisions be made on organizing their operating management team.

At present it is not yet viable and realistic for the foreign investors to localize their senior management team of their Chinese business, considering the shortage of qualified Chinese executives in the market. Such disadvantage would last for a decade or so before the younger generation of the Chinese people will finally be capable of taking up greater responsibilities in large corporations in the merciless business world.

At the moment it is advisable that if there is no qualified versatile executives and managers to fill in the heavyweight management positions in your Chinese operation, foreign investors should consider if it is more viable to postpone their project schedule or at least cut the project down to size a little to sustain the risks on an acceptable level. After all, a late arrival at a new market could no longer put you in an inferior position as it was like before, and the market is much less resistant to new entry as it was too.

## Real cost saving

One of key advantages for a localization of your organization, especially the management team, is to lower the overhead and consequently reduce operating cost, and it is one of the convenient ways to improve the annual financial reports when the business has been not quite in a good shape.

In the first place as said before, if you are not quite sure if the right-hand man of your choice is the right person to take up a vital role in commanding your thousand-mile-away Chinese business, you had better give it a second thought and review again the whole feasibility study of such business. Either you should downsize the scale of your investment, or at least slow down the rollout of your China project a little. A decision made with a naïve thought that vacancies of senior position can be filled with the available and yet only the second best team would end up the business with a disastrous result.

Similarly, if you are not sure if the replacement could deliver better done jobs to you, senior management positions should not change hands too frequent in order not to inference or lose the continuation of your business development in progress. In addition, it should also be taken into account if your local organization as a whole would adjust itself to such kind of re-organization. A typical organization composed of mainly Chinese people would easily breed factions inside the organization. There is a Chinese saying 'New emperor raises new officers and servants' which could best describe when the power at the top changes hand, a re-organization of the people and a change in their respective power in the structure would be foreseen. Though politics is usually the by-product in a group of three persons or more. However, in a typical Chinese organization it might need more than just masterful political skills to manage. Chinese people are accustomed to live with these struggles in their daily lives and they are probably much less concerned than the stakeholders of the company about that the factious conflicts or factious disagreement might be fatal to the quality of team work and work efficiency.

It is not uncommon that a joint venture company owned by a foreign investment would have named three general managers in succession within five years and yet is unable to turn around their dying business slightly. It could be attributed that in many cases the poor performance of an investment in China cannot be just one individual's fault and therefore a replacement of individual managers cannot revive your tarnished business unless a more radical move would be made such as a removal of the whole management team or an exercise of re-engineering process.

Localization should not be viewed as a means to reduce cost and even though it may be considered appropriate actions at certain stage of your business development, the decision should be taken from a perspective of organizational behavior instead of financial viewpoint alone.

## Lifetime expatriation

Many expatriates have been seconded in its current capacities in China for years and they should have gained very valuable experiences in China market. This in return let them contribute even more into building the business and developing the companies into new era. Is it so?

Many multinational companies seem not have long-term career development plans for their individual expatriates in their Chinese operation. And expatriate executives and managers are staying in China long enough to start to suspect if they are going to stay there forever. It is not as easy as one would think for a foreigner to stay and work in China for years, compared with those working in other Asian countries like Japan or Thailand. They would find that they are in a sense isolated from the local community, there are not many people who they meet everyday would speak foreign languages, their quality of life is down-graded in this less developed country, they are probably loaded with stress in their daily challenging works and etc.

Before long, some of these once-career-minded expatriates would be totally worn-out at the devastating business situation and lose their enthusiasm in growing the business as if it was unavoidable.

Some others would start to seek personal interests for compensation. They do not care if the business in China can survive the next month, instead they are more concerned about if they are still entitled to similar remuneration packages plus other fringe benefits as of today twelve months later...

I personally think that an expatriate's contribution to the infant business in China will probably get more and more marginal as the business is evolving into the next stages. Provided that there are some qualities and abilities which you can find in many excellent business development executives and managers in common, a competent expatriate can make a big difference in the very beginning of a start-up business in China. However, when the business develops into the next stage, the organization will be in need of different kind of managers and executives who possess a different set of qualities and abilities to invigorate the business again. For instance, a risk taker with an analytical mind and sharp judgment would turn to be a qualified candidate for a job of business executive whereas a good organizer with meticulous attention and management skills would be the right person to success a preliminarily established business and 'tune' the components of the whole business for further development.

It may be a wise idea for the foreign investors to devise some reasonable repatriation programs for their expatriates who are now working in China and in the meantime develop an appropriate performance appraisal system which can enable the headquarters to communicate with their outbound senior staff and identify any hidden difficulties faced by them in their work in China, for the mutual benefits of both parties.

## Organizing a merged team

Many multinational corporations have tremendous experiences in handling corporate acquisition and merger around the world. In a project of corporate merger, it always involves merging two or more organizations of different backgrounds together.

If managing people can be said a subject in science, managing people skillfully can be one of an art.

Some foreign investments in their first time of entering Chinese market would have been very busy with their teams of lawyers on the stacks of legal documents or a bunch of financial advisors on various estimates and projection on earning potential, and pitifully neglect the importance of designing a viable organizational structure and deployment of people until the last minute when it is needed urgently. At last, a poor-deployed organization by hurried decisions on your China project turns out to be a subtle cause for lot of future troubles.

Chinese people are most accustomed to rely on collective leadership and they expect the management to be a cohesive team and able to exercise their leadership effectively. A cohesive management team at the top or an image of cohesion they are projecting will be one of the best stimuli that can stabilize and further motivate the people below on each level to work in the direction to enhance the well being of the company as a whole. Nevertheless, it is usually the weakest aspect that most foreign investments in China are doing to establish cohesive management team, for their management teams most likely consist of members of different ethnics, languages, cultures, values and so forth. Without a strong and collaborative management team at the top, the performance of a Chinese organization would deteriorate very quickly, much quicker than one would imagine as in an organization of westerners in the west.

In addition, an informal and flat organization structure would be an viable alternative to speed up the communication process between levels, encourage the information sharing among departments, promote team spirit and etc., not to mention management could easier be alerted with emerging problems and be responsive fast to changes.

## Transfer of technology and know-how

It is a misunderstanding that the main job for expatriates sent to China by foreign investments is to dedicate their unique know-how and experiences in their capacities and get the jobs better done. It is evident at present that there are lots of areas where you cannot find in the local job markets many local Chinese who can capably meet the specific job requirements and take the challenges with own experiences or knowledge. An expatriate incumbent in these cases is the only choice. However, it is not in the best interests of the foreign investments if they merely expect their expatriate staff to fulfill the job requirements and undervalue their potential roles in training up the local talents to succeed the business in the long run. It is not only a matter of cost but also a challenge to your business expansion inside this big country.

Only those foreign investors who have the visions and commitment on the subject of transfer of experiences and know-how from expatriates to local managers would be able to make the best use of their human resources and grasp every opportunity of growth.

## Who manages the business?

Here we are not talking about whether the local business should be managed by an expatriate management team or a team composed of local Chinese. These two management models are not mutually exclusive and instead more likely have a sequential relationship. Starting with the former in the business in the early stages and then gradually it may transform into the latter model when it appears appropriate and necessary.

Specifically speaking, some foreign investments have an intention of letting their expatriate team blueprint and afterwards install a 'management system' in their Chinese business and expect such system would facilitate them to remotely manage the local organization and steer the businesses. Such practice would work if and only if their people were robot-like and their behaviors are strictly predictable. Many foreign investments are relying on numerous weekly reports or overviews in fancy or complicated format, powerful top-graded computerized management systems of millions' worth, teleconferencing for hours across the oceans everyday, pages after pages of authorization procedures and so forth, in their operation in China in order to straighten their businesses. It in reality seems not as constructive as they are supposed in many cases, as far as efficiency or effectiveness are concerned.

A system is static and neutral and error-free until 'people' is involved and interacted with it. The combination will make your Chinese business as a whole full of uncertainties, unpredictability, biases, and errors unless you have the right persons to ensure they are minimized to the lowest level whenever possible.

To dream of a 'system' that could have worked very fine with and for a bunch of average people should be left to academic discussions of scholars and philosophers of management sciences. Instead of investing a king's ransom endlessly to create the best system in the world to bring about miracles, major efforts should be diverted into improving your people's management skills, professional knowledge, and basic qualities as a good employee. Perhaps, you need not find the best system yourself and they can already build one for you in return.

# Good connection with authorities places you in fast track

'Guangxi' as word in Chinese with meaning of connection, is the word, which would best describe the first lesson that a foreign investor would learn in his first visit to China.

If the multinational corporation you are working for is famous enough, you would possibly be impressed by the hospitality and courtesy presented not only by your local business partner but also the bunch of officials from local authorities. You would then realize how intensively the state or local government would get involved in the commercial activities that in your home country might be strictly 'commercial' under the motto of capitalism. Very soon though the courteous acquaintances and the subsequent connections you or your local partner have established with these officials would prove to be worthwhile your time around the dining tables and entertainment expenses, when you are anxiously in critical moments in search of external helping hands to clear some obstacles in your way. However, you should be aware of the fact that everything has its limit and you need not be so dependent on external helping hands and push them to the limit.

## Marathon wrestling with authorities of all levels

It is well-known fact there are always conflicts of interest between local government and central government in China as there are everywhere else. You are supposed to obtain a very good understanding on whom you are talking to and should be talking to every time you are having some problems. It is not an easy task of getting to understand the basics, since the span of control, authorities and responsibilities are very complicated for the countless local authorities in the whole bureaucracy and the complication is doubled as far as corresponding bodies and authorities from central government are concerned. It appears highly likely beyond the understanding of most local Chinese, not to mention for a foreigner like you.

Inevitably, you are in need of some experts in this area and it is probably your local business partner could help you out here, or some legal advisors who have had proven track record specializing in this field. A good advisor on this issue would be able to shred a light on your problems on hand regarding legal matters, and when and from which government authority you are supposed to raise the enquiries to and seek resolutions.

There have been numerous examples that when a deal is nearing to be closed then the whole project would be hanging in the air as it is interfered by a higher authorities from the central government and finally the project would end up evaporating gradually without a trace.

The word of wisdom is not to rely completely on the local government on crucial matters and always prepare yourself to some sudden changes in decided matters since they might be higher authorities from central government who has the power to overrule what have been agreed between you and your well acquainted local authorities now and then. It is advisable that there is only one true rule you can take for granted, and it is 'there are always exceptional cases which can be handled differently from the common rules'. Sometimes this rule would be in your favor and sometimes not.

You should get used to the norm that the officials you are meeting would behave to either extreme; either they would promise everything you ever ask or hesitate to leak a 'yes' or 'alright' from his month the whole meeting. On either occasion you will learn quickly enough to assess the trustworthiness of individual officials.

All in all, partnering with your own legal advisors who are experienced in China trade would be a good strategy to get along with your Chinese business partners as well as the government officials of various authorities on every level. Your connection would be a valuable asset to your investment and its future but you cannot cling the future of your business entirely to a few promises or commitment made by your acquaintances under any circumstances.

The bright side of this topic is that Chinese government has been trying to streamline its redundant and bulky bureaucracy, enhance the quality of its civil servants, patch the loopholes in its legal system, and separate government officials from active involvement into commercial activities in the business sector, so that you are going to meet more and more professional civil servants who are strictly 'playing' by the rules and regulations and laws.

## Authority disproportional to ranking

Your connections with some big shots on high level would not be helpful when a decision in agreement with the top authorized persons comes to the operating episodes in the routine daily work. It might be one of the typical characteristics you would ever find in all bureaucracy of inefficiency.

Surely many foreign investments have been taught lessons on having hard times in their daily business when some low-ranking civil servants are making troubles to them. You would be surprised at some stories of which a project of million's worth is delayed because a form of some kind is stuck in the hands of the clerk for days, and you would be much more surprised at the fact that as you would see, he will receive not at all punishment in any form for his misdemeanor or mistake, until later you are told he is actually a nephew of Mr. So-and-so, a relative of the deputy mayor and therefore…Of course the top bosses of those foreign investments will never know this to be happening every-day in their sub-ordinate's daily working lives, however, these will unavoidably dampen your smooth daily operation of the business somehow, usually at the critical moments.

One of the viable solutions would be an establishment of a small taskforce or division who is responsible for coordinating all kind of public relations activities with external bodies, especially government-related matters and by doing so, you would centralize the effort and time to deal with each party of this 'customer' with 'tailor-made' services. The aim is to build up a closer relationship with individuals and ease your staff's daily contact with these people.

## You as the supporting cast

On many occasions are there big bosses from both sides attending a negotiation or a meeting and these chances always present themselves when a courteous visit is paid and the last time when a critical decision would have to be made by both sides. As a norm in the west, in such kind of business meetings the big bosses will host the meeting and manage the talking dominantly most the time. On the contrary, in China it seems that the big bosses are usually passing on the chairing position to his right-hand men and prefer playing guest. Moreover, it seems evident that the more important the occasion is, the more likely they act this way.

It would be a norm but it seems more like a typical tactic for a Chinese boss in power who would master to deal with his business acquaintances.

A foreigner if understanding this basic manner would follow this norm and delegate properly his authorities to his second-in-command to handle the discussions on his behalf. Further it would help to avoid lots of misunderstanding caused by language barrier and reserve some flexibility in your negotiations, if you have a reliable deputy who could command Chinese language and possess experiences in China trade, especially on critical topics in relation to the business. Only when serious matters are rising for patching and repairing, the top persons can stand out and address the problems face to face.

# A deliberate national marketing plan will prevail

As said before, the management team of a newly established business tends to be in pursuit of sales turnover as it would be the primary objective to measure the performance of the company and subsequently that of the team itself, in addition to some common financial performance measures such as profitability, return on investment and etc. In other cases, some multinational corporations are more likely to measure the productivity of a business in a way that its share of the market is the focal criterion.

In China, it would be difficult for the foreign investments to measure their market share on a basis of reliable raw data of objectivity, for the reason of the absence of active industry-recognized market research firms and the unavailability of reliable and complete market data in the nation at present. A multitude of factors have made sales turnover the most convenient element to measure the company's overall performance.

This way of thinking fits into the conventional Chinese's way of doing business since Chinese businessmen are used to see 'sales turnover' as the most crucial indicator to the healthiness of their business. Their modest attention to the implications of inventory level and credit control on the corporate financial position has led to a nationwide economic crisis the past decades. In the old days of plan economic system with production-driven commercial activities, most state run enterprises have been taught tough lessons but old habits are hard to kill. The undergoing economic reform and restructuring of state owned enterprises are step-by-step reviving many state run companies, however, it is still a long bumpy road to go to catch up with the western world.

Besides, plenty of Chinese companies are consistently so overwhelmed by the sales-driven mindset that it blurs their perception of what marketing management is really about. If it could be more likely that many global companies in the west would structure their organization in a way that marketing function is overseeing the sales function, many Chinese companies would have a tendency to do just the opposite. To the majority of many Chinese companies and their managers, marketing management may entail merely a statement of definition of target market, plus some activities of advertising and promotion of their products or services, and most importantly a budget of tidy sum to manage. The lack of in-depth knowledge of how modern marketing management would enhance their businesses, leads to their reluctance to found a marketing function of privilege inside the companies and govern the business direction and strategic planning on the overall business.

To better divide the jobs between each party of the joint venture companies of the foreign investor and local partner and make the best use of their own expertise in different business areas, an organization is always composed of a marketing department headed by expatriate director and the sales function led by a Chinese sales director in many cases. Ironically, not many global corporations would stand any possibilities of letting their marketing function be a lame duck while their Chinese partners appear doubtful with the existence of such 'big spending' department. Here come all kinds of conflict of interest and office politics.

In case sales function and marketing function should fail to share common views and work closely together, needlessly to say, the hostile relationship between these two heavyweight departments will probably drain the healthy business away to a hopelessness.

Though, the above mentioned does not necessarily mean that a business equipped with superior marketing function over the sales function is a problem-free set-up to run the business in China. There are still some very successful multinational companies in which sales-driven organizational structures are adopted.

## Who is who?

To determine who is who in your business in China, it depends on the natures and characteristics of the particular industry a business belongs to.

In simple words, the level of your dependence on marketing function to build up a prosperous business is greatly subject to the fact that you are marketing your products and services in mass consumer market or in an industrial market. The spectrum of nature of target market will determine if you should employ a marketing-driven organization or not. The current trend of an integration of individual sales function into marketing function would be a viable alternative in order to keep all of your sales efforts in line with the overall marketing objectives of the companies in servicing the mass market where you need appropriate effective marketing strategies, plans and activities to communicate with your potential customers. On the contrary, in industrial market, a sales-driven organization would better help you understand the specific needs articulated by individual customers with competent account servicing with your customers at the center of your attention. In the latter cases, marketing measures are customized to facilitate the sales efforts.

Foreign investors in China should therefore decide which kind of organizational structure would better suit their business and fit people into the positions in the first place. In the meantime, it is recommended to integrate both functions together and avoid a presumption that expatriate can do better jobs in a marketing capacity and Chinese will in a sales capacity.

Marketing management was definitely invented in the west and so far many Chinese managers and executives are yet in a learning stage in this area, to be frank. Though if it is agreeable that a precise under-standing of local market environment and its customers, their tastes, their specific needs, their behavior patterns and etc., would be a requisite for sensible and exquisite marketing management, a local talent in marketing capacity to assist your expatriate marketing manager should be worth serious consideration, as far as a synergy effect of market understanding of local Chinese and marketing expertise of your expatriate marketing experts is concerned.

Besides, it is wise not to build up 'invisible walls' between your sales team and marketing team by a common mistake that many foreign investments are committing easily. This 'invisible wall' is a consequence of a tendency that many expatriate crews are assigned into marketing capacities when sales position holders are mainly Chinese. Its existence blocks the communication and information flow easily, though unnecessarily, and breeds conflicts and politics as far as different cultures and languages and experiences are concerned. If possible, a good mixture of expatriate staff with local staff in every individual department would ease the possible daily conflicts and the most important but least mentioned advantage is to produce an working environment in which best experience transfer and exchange of ideas can be achieved by coaching and learning of every party.

## Trade marketing is the key

Trade marketing is a sub-function of marketing management function to facilitate sales development by on-the-spot promotional activities along the distribution network of your products or services. In the west trade marketing is so well established that it becomes more or less routine automated efforts diverted in the distribution processes. Compared with advertising on mass media, trade marketing is a supplementary tool to the former and normally it is granted a much smaller budget every year.

However, as its name has implied, trade marketing is some promotional tools that a company could devise in association with or for the trade partners and intermediaries in the distribution channel with an aim to induce demands on its products or services. In most industries other than those conglomerates who are delivering its products and services strictly on their own without any intermediaries between themselves and their customer, trade marketing is the only media to let you meet and interact with your consumers and customers.

Considering the fact that distribution network in China appears a restrictive system in many industries in a sense of limited number of channel type, lack of network of nation-wide coverage, relative dominance of state controlled channels, complex legal constraints against free trading activities, inefficiency of existing supply chain management, and etc., I would see that trade marketing is far more an important determinant factor which can affect how successful a company can promote its products and services and add as much value as possible into the existing business, than it is now in the western world.

Those who can, to maximum extent, manipulate or collaborate with its distributing agents and intermediaries including wholesalers and retailers in the network would more likely win a bigger share of the market over their competition.

Believing it or not, when many foreign investors are investing like billionaires in mass media advertising in China with a high hope they will be ultimately rewarded with higher brand awareness, impressive top-of-mind recall rate, tripled sales turnover, or growing share of market, it is extremely difficult to measure the cost effectiveness of their advertising and promotion spending every year in their real lives in China. It is because it requires manning your team heavily to just monitor the progress and collect market feedback from such a geographically big market as China. In addition, it is yet not practical to delegate the jobs to your intermediaries in the business processes since you are probably dealing with a large number of customers who are not familiar with this kind of management practices. If so, eventually you might only have bits and pieces of incomparable and useless data and information all over your office. Neither are there so far reliable third-party research houses in the neighborhood that would serve you with a nation-wide coverage and deliver to you with tons of remarkable data and information at your arm's length timely, as you may have expected in a well-developed market.

It is actually like a shoot in the dark when a media budget is approved since you never know whether and how your corporate image, your brands, your products or services are benefited from your decisions. Your have to rely on your expertise and experiences and sometimes your hunches, to guide your decisions in this 'black box' operation and hope that somehow your are winning more and more sales orders day by day.

To resolve this situation that would remain a very challenging one in the foreseeable future, a foreign investor is in need of an excellent operations management to optimize your routine trade marketing activities and each specific campaign in execution. Great ideas in promotion would be killed by one minor mistake after another in the implementation stage, and the frequency of occurrence of such is much higher in a market where many controllable factors turn out to be uncontrollable and known risks become unknown.

Despite of all these scary limitations, trade marketing is in my opinion, yet the most powerful tool to win the competition in China, in the sense of cost effectiveness.

Each big city in China can be viewed as an independent market for foreign investments and they ought to be treated differently. The attributes of active local partners, distribution network, business practices, legal requirements, and competition, market situation and consumer behaviors differentiate from each other in each region and province in China. A reminder to yourself and your organization of this will only do good to your more sensible decision making in your China project. Occasionally a costly nation-wide mass media advertising campaign may be helpful in case of critical project such as product re-launch, or brand re-positioning in China, however, it is trade marketing that a success in implementing a trade marketing campaign will not only bring in immediately more shelf off-take and sales orders but also set up a scenario in which you are meeting with your consumers and customers intensively.

As mentioned, trade structure in China is dominated by very a few retailers in each major city in China, some of them are a faction of local conventional yet self-evolving retailers and the other is the quickly emerging global retailing giants. They might run their businesses in a very different way but they definitely share one idea in common–'once you are offering shelf space for sale, you are the king'. Moreover, Chinese consumers are not having many alternatives in knowing your brands and your products, they are very likely to get to know your companies, brands and products in the shops and only in the shops. Very often your local trade partners will remind you of that it is time for you to spend some money to run some kind of trade activities or you are going to lose some sales, and your shelves. It is a matter of how well you may collaborate with your local trade partners, how effectively you can manage the trade marketing activities, and how productive you can interact with your consumers and customers through the series of these activities.

Trade marketing in China is not an easy job for foreign investors since you are supposed to have a very capable trade marketing team, which can plan meticulously and manage effectively and efficiently the details on run-down of each operational activities in a lots of sites across the territory simultaneously, and work closely with your local trade partners of whatever types. However, those who can manage to do so consistently are going to stand up to the challenges of the consumers and the competition.

## Investment and resource allocation region-wise

It is typical for foreign investments that a headquarters is established in one of the top cities in the territory of the market to oversee the overall business operation in China, except a few of those who still hold a fancy that a headquarters in Hong Kong or Asia Pacific region would still be able to work to the same effect.

As a matter of fact though, it is not enough having a headquarters inside Mainland China to steer your Chinese business if the daily operation of your business is strictly centralized in the headquarters, since this approach is not indeed far ahead of having a headquarters in Hong Kong or nearby Asian countries.

A common understanding on business sector in China is to divide the whole market into five to six regions, namely, northeast, central north, northwest, eastern, central region, southwest and south. It is a conventional method derived from the homogeneities of the grouping of provinces in terms of market situation, distribution channel, consumer behaviors, and etc., and still a workable access for foreign investments to plot their overall business strategies in the very beginning. Resources ought to be planned and allocated on a regional basis and it is more than just setting up your local organizations here. A deliberate regional plan on resources allocation in the business planning stage might look very costly in the short run, but it would solidify your business region by region in a way that an advertising budget of 'king's ransom' would not result in a drop in the ocean if these regional plans are to be carried out effectively.

Of course, you do not rush into all the regions and are going to develop the regions one by one lest you and your management team in the headquarters should get lost very soon when problems arise in all the regions simultaneously. In particular, certain degree of decentralization of your management and daily operations can lessen the stress on the headquarters and release it from non-core business issues day to day.

A network of regional management offices deployed in the regions is necessary to assist your daily management and disseminate correctly and thoroughly the decisions in the headquarters to the local organizations in the first place. In addition, this local network can therefore play a role in adapting headquarters' decisions in the light of their acquired experiences and knowledge of the local market attributes.

The last but not least, it is cautioned that such decentralization of management entails your controlling efforts to be placed on each regional management office to ensure they are not sidetracking and endangering the business and necessitate some versatile management staff to oversee your outbound operations.

## *Regional business plan*

When many foreign investments have made up their minds in investing into China, the next step is to mobilize all the resources and expertise to deliberate a business plan that could best enable them to kick off their execution of China project. However, most business plans are plotted by taking into considerations of the whole market and its trend, without a concrete idea whether and when and which region to start with. It is not practical at all to presume a nation-wide market coverage within the first one to two years since before long you will find more than enough reasons to justify a strategy of concentration into some primary regions instead of spreading your resources all over the territory.

If things are done wisely, there are high possibilities that your business can bear fruit upon only a few affluent provinces where you can identify correctly and capture successfully the local market demand on your products and services. It is not necessary for your business in China to cover the whole territory in order to achieve break-even at the bottom-line. On the contrary, it appears that the wider market coverage a business in China is targeting, the higher possibility it burns out its limited resources too early to reshape itself. 'Think big' is a good way to envisage the long-range prospect of your company and remain your focus of your business development, but it is very often not suitable for encompassing your daily management efforts and resource allocation.

If one can abandon the idea of China as a big market composed of four provincial municipals and thirty plus provinces and replace it with a concept of regions, it may be the right direction to start with in the process of business planning. One must bear in mind that economies of scale do not necessary offer you a quick and viable solution here in China. It may sound attractive to you that increase in production and full utilization of facilities will bring about decrease in production cost per unit, and consequently lower pricing policy and/or higher profit margin. In reality, it is true that you are able to reduce the pure production cost to certain extent, unfortunately, your cost saving will be offset by piling up of finished goods and raw materials, unbearably high costs in logistics, shortage of cash flow and incapability of handling a variety of local markets in case contingencies arise in the market environment somewhere, especially an unexpected change in competitive environment.

Consequently a full set of regional plans can at least underline when and how to initiate, develop and control your local business and a failure in executing a particular regional plan will not pose a significant threat to the other plans so that risks are assessed and controlled in your own hands.

# Advertising is the king

There are some well-known examples in the past decade that some multinational corporations were successful for they dared to impose a 'push' approach in developing the market and promote their business by heavy advertising and promotion. However, there have also been many firms among these foreign investments who are failing to advance themselves to a profitable business as planned after big spending on advertising resulting in poor market responses year after year. The reasons vary but in many cases, it can be concluded that a lack of in-depth understanding on the market, the consumers, and the environment does compel poor execution of these advertising and promotion programs and cause depreciation in impact of these campaigns and activities on the market in China.

## Advertising is a waste of resource?

Advertising is always a good tactic to have a new market developed in a short period of time for a company since a series of TV commercials or above-the-line advertising in other forms can, if they are executed properly to its target group, draw attention and induce trial in the market. The same theory can be applied in Chinese market. Therefore, you will find nowadays there are lots of local companies in various sizes in China who are more than willing to spare a huge sum in their annual budget on different kind of advertising and promotion and you see more commercials aired and outdoor billboards hoisted up by local brands of products and services than those by some global players, which are supposed to be more generous and anxious to spend money.

It is a general impression given to the business sector in China that Chinese consumers are relatively more easily and instantly influenced by advertising and promotion activities than those in the well-developed market, as far as sales figures in the promotional period are concerned. Numerous examples in China in the past decades have proven this hypothesis. It is true that Chinese consumers tend to welcome very much all kinds of promotional tools and advertising ideas and they are easily attracted and motivated to try the products and services if possible, especially in mass market of fast moving consumable products. Similarly, on-the-spot promotional activities are the next effective tools to induce patronages.

Hence, most advertising and promotional efforts would produce at least short-term and instant positive impact on your sales turnover and shelf off-take, since Chinese consumers are anxious to getting a hold of new information, new products, new applications, and etc. in their daily lives. They are also eager to absorbing the messages conveyed in your commercials, memorizing the new features of your products, and then diffusing it with their peers, family, neighborhood and even colleague in the workplace. That is because by tradition Chinese people value relatively the concept of 'family', 'community' and 'social life' more important than many other people in other countries, and they like to share their views and exchange ideas with the others in their everyday lives. With such social culture and norm, Chinese consumers will be actively and voluntarily promoting your products and services if they have a trial on them and are satisfied with their features and benefits. But at the same time, they could also cast a fatal threat by bad-mouthing your products and services if they do not stand up to their perceived expectation over them.

Chinese people are very accustomed to follow other people's thinking and behaviors in their daily consumption activities. If you see an over-crowded store where a sea of Chinese people rushing into the sales counters, two facts can probably be observed: first, the people there are probably belong to some families, or many of them are actually relatives, friends or neighbors; second, the product that they are looking for on shelves is probably at the moment heavily advertised in the television or so.

It can be a very interesting topic for social scientists to study why and how Chinese collectively behave in particular ways in their social life, though it is beyond our discussion here. All in all, testimonials and word of mouth are basically the most effective means to promote or demote something in China and the marketing practitioners should not underestimate its impact on the way that the general public would perceive your products and services and the way that they will respond to you will incredibly have a direct relationship with your sales performance.

The challenge here is that merely a bunch of money in your advertising budget sometimes cannot ascertain testimonials and word of mouth on your products and services in your favor. On the contrary, it requires your marketing team to possess a good understanding on the market and it consumers, coupled with a touch of creativity in their execution of the marketing plan to enhance the influence on your target consumers. Otherwise, your unprecedented large marketing budget in China would still be expended to no avail.

## Regional A&P plan

At the early stage most foreign investments are unavoidably to centralize all their marketing planning processes of their Chinese business under the control of the marketing team situated in the headquarters. No matter whether you have local organization in the variety of regions in Chinese market, you should opt to divide the marketing plans into regional plan on a region-by-region basis and stick to this management model at the very beginning of your start-up. As said before, China is actually a grouping together of heterogeneous markets and consumers and requires customized marketing development approaches if you are expecting your marketing expertise and know-how gained in the west to be one of your core competencies in contrast to your competition in China.

Some might think that they can afford a full-service advertising agency and expect a close working relationship with the agency can dramatically ease the pressure from the daily operational difficulties in marketing their products and services in such a big country. However, so far there seems not any full-service advertising agency of international experiences that could have established their own 'nation-wide' connection or exposure across the territory to fulfill your urgent needs. Either they are right in their own episode of business development or they can only offer their services in specific top cities in China. Worse enough, they are always not able to bargain on your behalf for lowest media costs, compared with the substantially lower airtime charges offered by some local agencies. Surely the quality of latter's services would be incomparable with many international advertising agencies, however, it is noticeable that the advertising industry appears so far not well established as thought of to facilitate your marketing efforts very effectively. In my opinion, the situation will remain unchanged until the tight manipulation and interferences from the administration on the concerned industries will diminish gradually as the market-driven economy is better regulated by itself in a lawful and systematic manner in the long run.

Whether or not you can take advantages of your local partners' connection with local media or you can empower a network of outbound marketing teams of ability to execute your marketing plans, it is recommended that a regional plan for each primary market defined in terms of region should be formulated and well communicated internally across the disciplines and externally with your distribution network and your advertising agencies. If possible, advertising agencies of stronger local market exposure and coverage and with richer experiences in Chinese market could be more valuable to your success in planning, executing and controlling your marketing activities throughout the courses of your business.

In addition, local intermediaries of your distribution network such as wholesalers and traders would be able to make the best use of their local connection with local medias for you and therefore proper delegation of authorities and responsibilities in this regard could be worthwhile considering by many foreign investments, since they can bring in real cost saving on your operation to great extent.

As a matter of fact, many of the foreign investments are reluctant to believe that there can be mutual trust between themselves and their Chinese partners and it normally takes much longer time than it should in other Asian countries for them to start thinking that their Chinese partners are trustworthy and capable of performing their roles. It might be the subtle but long-lasting effect of the 'sleeping dragon' image adhered to this ancient country of long histories.

There may be 'terrible' stories and rumors of foreign investments in experiences with some cunning Chinese business partners and ending up in miserable doom somewhere down the market now and then. However, when they cannot suppress their fear of the fact that their Chinese business partners might play tricks against them if they are allowed to get too much involved into their internal daily operations, you are actually the only ones who can initiate the building up mutual trusting relationship with your Chinese partners.

One must not expect that their local Chinese partners would take the initiatives first since a typical Chinese seems very likely skeptical in every foreigner until he has taken his time understanding him well enough to reward him his trust in him. This mentality and way of thinking are everywhere in the Chinese business world, as an old Chinese idiom says 'Business is warfare in nature' and it is matter of life and death.

It should be one of the top priorities for the foreign investors to earn the trust from his local business partners and other stakeholders at the very beginning and maintain this mutually trusting relationship successfully because mutual trust is the key facet of 'local connection' by which you can be spared from lots of unnecessary troubles and problems day after day in your business in China.

Hence, it is not so farfetched as many foreign investors might have been thinking that they could build up and maintain a very close and harmonious working relationship with their local Chinese partners, the key is to adopt the right approach in the very beginning and earn their trust. Once it is achieved, the rewards from your partner would be as promising as you may obtain elsewhere in the western business world, in the saving of promotional costs alone would be worth trying some efforts.

## Product is the hero

What could be more fascinating than that a successful advertising campaign is rewarded by a consequential doubled sales turnover as targeted, in the eyes of the top management of a company who is aggressive enough to slice 40% of its gross profit margin into advertising and promotion budget for a year. Yet, this might not be something you as one of the members in the management team could have imagined nowadays in the western market where most your fellow competitors are backing up their business with above-the-line supports of a terrific budget month after month. However, in a rapidly developing market such as China it is highly plausible and possible to be one of the real legendary stories in the business sector, an excellent campaign of TV commercials to draw immediate mass attention and appeal the mass to wait right before the shelves for your products the weeks to come.

Bombing the market with a series of above-the-line promotional activities would be the best shortcut to overtake your competition and win the market quickly in China and this market situation would remain the same in the years to come. Nevertheless, it is not a master key to achieve and attain your success, if a foreign investment does not have its own core competencies to out-compete the market, other than a mouth-watering budget on advertising and promotion every year.

The most pathetic type of competition in the business world is the one that all the participants are only spending their last dime on large-scale promotion with a fantasy of monopolizing the market by elimination of other players in the first place. It turns out to be a game of 'who is richer'. Lessons are taught in the industries of high technologies and internet service where people are now painfully learning a hard fact that money cannot always buy them the market and those who fails to deliver their products and services up to the needs of the market will be forgotten and disappear right at the moment they burn out all their money unproductively.

Since there always come new players in the industry that you belong in such a new and big market, your business in China is continuously exposed to new competition threatening to take over your position everyday. It would happen when a new comer is fuelling his own business with a great deal of resources in advertising and promotion to march in the marketplace, and one must beware of the fact that Chinese consumers are rather irresistible to this type of marketing strategies and easily influenced in their behavioral patterns accordingly. The best approach to defense your business from assault is to concentrate on how to create the best value of your products and services to best meet the needs of your consumers and customers.

Analogically speaking, advertising would be said as the king, as it powers up you and your company to overwhelm in the market in an instant, it might not result in an outcome as desired. In the contrast, I would prefer my belief of one of the traditional values embodied in many successful multinational corporations in their respectively industries, 'product is the hero'. It is always a hero who would re-write the histories and likewise, it is only the added value of your products and services created by you and your company that can make a lifelong difference in the future of your business and the return on your investment in China.

## Marketing talents in China

Marketing management is a body of professional and practical knowledge that has been developed for several decades in the western business world and it has a broader scope of knowledge in which sales management is regarded as merely a key component of the overall marketing management.

I could still remember that marketing as a set of professional knowledge was not yet well recognized, and far from as popular as it is now, in the years of eighties in Hong Kong, one of the best internationalized cities in Asia, which has been famous for its free market economy then. People were more accustomed to putting their management efforts on subjects in direct relation to selling. Understanding on marketing management was then rather primitive and limited in a sense that marketing management was simply working on some print materials of informative nature for circulation; erection of some outdoor billboards for market presence; or production of cheap premiums like calendar or so for give-away, etc. and all these marketing tactics were supposed to facilitate their core activity of their business: selling.

This ways of thinking in doing business still embody the mainstream mentality of prevailing generations of many Chinese businessmen and executives at the present time, even though they have been benefited from tremendous exchanges of best experience in marketing management in the past decades. The positive side of this story is that many young Chinese executives are quick learners on modern management concepts and knowledge and they are receiving better on-the-job training than ever from their personal experiences with big corporations of foreign investment the past years. However, are on-the-job trainings sufficient to develop a Chinese fresh graduate into a skilled and proficient marketing manager and let him run marketing discipline capably? I am afraid the answer is not.

The challenge here is that in China there is generally still a lack of high quality specialized academic trainings on business disciplines provided by local universities. The existing prospectus and curriculums in the majority of local universities are either behind the times and just simply not comparable to those of western business schools in terms of fitness to modern business world.

In China, you would easily identify a fresh graduate who possesses a promising academic background of finance or accounting and is proficient with local accounting practices, however, it is relatively much more difficult to hire someone from the college who would be versatile with skills of marketing management and pick up his jobs as quickly as expected, since the latter requires somehow the candidate to be more trained up in his college life, if not talented or gifted, with some specific attributes like creativity, business acumen and so forth.

At present there are many positions in marketing function that are actually filled by persons who were specializing instead in the field of technology or other business disciplines other than marketing management in their academic studies and their previous job capacities. It is not saying that a financial manager could definitely foul a job in marketing function, on the contrary, it is just that availability of good marketing executives with formal trainings on the subject would spare a lot of companies from wasting their time and efforts unnecessarily and venturing their businesses with unfit managers.

Relative scarcity of adept local marketing talents would be one of the top concerns for the foreign investment who are expanding their businesses into China, especially in a sense that Chinese market is such a volatile environment that a capable team of local marketing talents can positively add values to the entire local organization. If best experience transfer is ever needed between your local organization in China and your headquarters, a transfer in your marketing function would be the most needed one, as far as urgency of such needs is concerned. The most viable approach to go around this challenge would be a mixture of expatriate marketing staff with local ones under the supervision of a skilled marketing manager, mostly likely an expatriate, in order to achieve a synergy of professional expertise and local market knowledge.

In addition, as it might be neglected easily and not thought of by many foreign investment, it is important to allot a key member on each level of the marketing organization, managerial and operational level all together, and they are supposed to train and coach the local staff with their experiences, transfer over their skills and knowledge in a pre-defined period of time. This special taskforce could be a group of expatriate staff who specialize in their individual scope of job responsibilities, regardless of their ranking and importance of their works in the marketing function. That is because lot of failures in many foreign investments in Chinese market are not attributed to their poor decision-making or silly ideas, instead, many of them fail in the stage of execution and implementation of their plans and ideas. Very often these routine yet critical operational problems at the lower level of the organization are out of reach or even unknown to the persons in charge of the department.

Once this group of special taskforce is set in place to enhance the productivity of the entire marketing department in your local organization in China, the additional costs incurred in this regard will be justified by long-term interest to be gained by the whole business.

## Partnering with intermediaries

In a free market economy, you may have full latitude in manipulating your internal resources and picking up business partners of your choice that you have confidence in relying on them to develop your business hand-in-handedly.

Unfortunately it appears not the same kind of story in China as it is yet a market massively regulated by the administration visibly or invisibly and therefore you are supposed to abide by the laws and regulations in association with conducting business in China. Someone might say that here and there are so many loopholes in the system where one may take advantage and go around unfavorable situations somewhere sometime, however it cannot be a reliable strategy in the long run, especially under the circumstances which large amount of critical resources are involved in your implementing your specific plans in relation to marketing management. You cannot believe that your own team and own organization can address the daily headaches one by one without a need to outsource some helps from external parties. In every case you could have to extend your team spirit to include your various local business partners along the supply chain so as to navigate your business effectively.

It is not inventing a wheel to say that a solid and stable relationship with your local business partners throughout your supply chain would be very influential to your success in the market, but a good partnership with each of them can do you and your company in China a lot of good in several areas. The advantages are which you would hardly enjoy now in well-developed markets elsewhere and only here in China when it is still in the phases of transformation from plan-driven economy to market-driven economy. In these stages most local business and enterprises are more than willing to co-operate earnestly with their foreign partners since a good and stable relationship and connection is still a bread-and-butter business for them now. Until they are going to evolve into a modernized self-contained economic system and be strong enough to stand up to the international competition in the coming decades, their foreseeable future does cling heavily inevitably to their individual links to their foreign counterparts at present. They are anxious to your new technology, modern management skills, advance knowledge and know-how, and most important of all, your capital investment.

First of all, your local business partners are your interface to the local market, forming a nation-wide network of information collecting and disseminating. These information ranges from market trends to new local policies on commerce and so on. It can be one of the most understandable examples to illustrate the notion of 'information is power', and one's dominance in collecting information of various types in a semi-closed market can most likely let him stand in a favorable position in exclusive business opportunities now and then. As a matter of the fact that local policies and regulations vary in most provinces and cities, it requires more than that you just follow the rules and regulations published by central government from time to time. More importantly, your local business associates are highly likely connected to state or local authorities in one way or the other, and it enables them to grasp substantial key information of your interest all the time. Hence, it is far more cost efficient to integrate with this nation-wide interface into your own organization in this huge market than to try forming your own people on every spot where you have presence. It is my experiences that local partners can always come up with good ideas to help foreign investments tackle and resolve local issues of everyday business. With their input and advice, your people's main job can then be just to pick the 'right' solution in the best interest of your company.

Secondly, a good relation with local business partners can in many cases, enable your business to monopolize the local market in a sense of which they are willing to team up with you on a firmer basis at the expense of other business opportunities presented in the competitive environment if they are convinced that it is in their best interest. You should bear in mind the fact that so far the channel of supply chain across the territory, including the physical distribution channel such as wholesalers and retailers, is yet a channel of fixed and highly regulated structure in which you do not have many alternatives as you do elsewhere. Once certain available resources in the supply chain in your particular industry are occupied by one of the core player inside, it will to great extent substantiate the difficulties for others to squeeze in and take its share easily without extraordinary efforts than usual.

Thirdly, partnering with local business associates would considerably cut down your internal organization to size that would reduce your operating cost as much as possible at the start-up stage and even the later ones. Overhead costs in operating the business for a foreign investment in China would be above-averagely higher than what they are experiencing in their market elsewhere. Very often, they have a tendency to simply expand their local organization at a high pace whenever they feel that workloads are multiplying day after day, with a temptation of low labor cost in China and therefore they are declined to mistakenly overstaff themselves to boost up efficiency. Before long, the ever expanding organization and its subsequent increase in overhead costs will be eating up their gross profit bit by bit year by year. The misconception of low labor cost in China has driven many foreign investors into a trap that they unconsciously raise their policies on compensation and benefit to hire high caliber local staff or simply allow themselves to take higher than planned head count in their organizations to run their businesses. Unfortunately an increase in head count is not just a matter of a budget of salaries since it has a serious implication on overall administrative costs like office space, pensions, meal allowances, transportation and etc. There is no doubt why many foreign investments that are estimated to produce a gross profit of 50% or more are yet running their business at a substantial operating loss. Therefore, if you can make the best use of your local business partners in the sense of cost saving, you could successfully downsize your own organization and get rid of lots of unnecessary overhead costs. They may spare you their idling manpower to take up lots of field jobs and it could just cost you at a fixed rate every month for a long period of time. It is worthwhile considering for those front-line jobs such as sales support, merchandising, trade marketing coordination, and even stock keeping and so forth.

Operations management should be the focus for foreign managements as far as low operating productivity and business ineffectiveness are concerned. In this regard, your local business associates throughout the supply chains would be the answer to your question of how to optimize your daily business operation and heighten its productivity in the long run.

# The defeated die of unfavorable market situation

Most people are more interested in others' stories of failure and keep on reading these sad stories from time to time in business journals and magazines. The latter of course is more than willing to satisfy the curiosities of the general public by repetitively publishing pages after pages of how some famous foreign investors are 'learning' painfully the rules of game here or simply how some other big world-class players have ended up in a poor shape in their long adventures in this ancient country. Their stories are precisely explored or properly exaggerated, and specified with background information, in addition to a conclusion of the likely cause of death or so. However, analyses are basically focused on one side of the story: foreign investors are suffering from the drastic adversities of China market and how they are interfered by the uncertainties in external environment of global politics, domestic economy and governmental administration from time to time. Here comes the question: are these big global players who are so experienced and sophisticated enough to dominate the global market for so many years would suddenly become that fragile to these threats posed internally in China market? What have made many of them who have succeeded in dealing with all kind of challenges elsewhere be so invulnerable here in China market and succumb to the domestic marketers easily?

It is true that in China political tensions in the international stage would have intensified the business climate now and then; or the ever-changing rules and regulations of the administration on commerce would have blurred your visions on your business development day by day; or the interference imposed by the administration to protect the domestic industries would have laden your China business with additional burdens, but how would it be different from the situation that most global players would have been in their past when venturing into overseas markets elsewhere?

Investing into some Southeast Asian countries would expose you to political risks, which are far more lethal than it would be in China for the past years. Similarly, constitutions on conducting business by foreign investments in many Asian countries are at least as complex as it has been in China. In addition, mindset of protectionism on domestic businesses is widely spread in the governments of many Asian countries across the Pacific Rim. The main difference between investing into China or elsewhere in Asia is two-folded: firstly, its vast market potential and its rewards are far more difficult to resist and secondly, direct investing into China intrinsically requires you to possess good understanding on the characteristics of this giant market and managerial competence to exploit it.

In many cases the management teams of most foreign investments would claim that adverse market situation should account for their failure to fulfill their business plans; and the fierce competitive environment in China market deters them from operating their businesses the way it would have been. Though it is to me that not many external factors should be the core determinant to a success of a foreign investment in China but the managerial competence of each particular firm. A foreign investor equipped with it could more likely excel the competition and can triumph in China market.

Any blame put solely on external problems by the executive management team of a foreign investment for their failure to grow their business in China as planned is probably prejudiced and, therefore a strong signal that the management is pitifully not honest to himself to the least. Their reluctance to recognize their weakness of management capabilities and to take firm remedial actions against it will only distress the situations inside and around the business further to the edge of abyss.

## Management philosophy and corporate culture

If you ask a top ranking executive of a global company about the corporate culture of his company or the management philosophy of his company, he would keep on talking sensibly for two hours and explaining articulately to you every detail since he is very likely very proud of it as he probably should. Many big companies are successful in their particular industries partly because they are capable of nurturing aligned corporate cultures across their organization on every level at every location and fostering team spirit among the majority of the members of the companies. It in return drives the majority of the organization to work hand-in-handedly to the common corporate objectives and attain the success of their entire businesses.

There is no doubt that you and your management team are looking forward to promoting in the local organization of your Chinese business certain values and norms endorsed and affirmed by the headquarters. These values and norms should on one hand be aligned with your global corporate cultures as a whole and on the other hand, form an ambience to unite together your local organization tightly.

Nevertheless, one's meat would be another's poison. In some cases, particular core values being shared by an organization in the workplace may enhance a drive of cohesiveness among the individuals and ultimately improve its productivity in the workplace, whereas the very same values would disjoin another organization and deteriorate its overall performance significantly. For instance, in western world individualism is regarded as a very common element in the everyday culture and it is translated into a fact that the employees are encouraged to working independently in his capacity and are delegated a leeway to maneuver his jobs with minimum supervision from his supervisor. However, if individualism would be concluded as partly a side-product of an affluent material world, as it could be stipulated by the theory of

Maslow's Hierarchy of Need, then Chinese society is far away from the state where individualism would be widely acknowledged gradually. Relying largely on their social connection with the communities, the majority of Chinese people are just simply not ready to alter their behavior patterns on collective basis in the working environment and place each of themselves in a position of an individual in a big organization.

Many big organizations are designing various programs and schemes in their companies to build up and promote corporate cultures of various kinds. However, culture is a feature that is intangible and difficult to observe or ascertain or maintain, especially when a group of people of diversified backgrounds is involved and the combination of the group is never static in the real world.

As a result, a try of importing your corporate cultures or management philosophy from the headquarters and enforcing it blindly without a closer look at your receiving party would be dangerous if they could ill fit into your local organization or your local staff do not have the aptitude to absorb and follow them adequately.

It does not mean that as a foreign investment you can spare any culture building programs such as team building technique, orientation on company history, exchange meeting with management and etc. from your local Chinese organization, on the contrary, Chinese people would very much welcome this kind of orientation and the result would be surprisingly positive if it is designed and executed triumphantly. It just requires that the same goals are to be done differently.

A sense of belonging to the company would be one of the key elements that may help you adhere your local Chinese organization tightly together and fight for the common objectives set by and for the company. When they feel like a member of the big family, they would totally dedicate to the company at their utmost without a second thought of the rewards they might ever get, and similarly, it they don't feel that way, their self-tolerance in substandard professional demeanor would consequentially endanger your daily operation far worse than you would expect in your western subsidiaries elsewhere.

All in all, a good understanding of Chinese mentality on work, their strength and weakness in character and the qualities and characteristics of Chinese as a people, can enable the foreign investors to better incorporate the overall corporate cultures and management philosophy into local needs of the local organizations and grant you the 'catalyst' to achieve synergistic effect of a group of individuals bonding together.

## Inexperience in starting from scratch

Obviously more and more global firms are looking at China as the biggest emerging market in the world for the decades to come, and many of them are also active advocates for China being set at high agenda in their strategic business planning now and then on many press occasions. When it is probably true that China has been in the spotlight of global business expansion, it appears that not many global corporations are actually incorporating their strategic move into this market with their globalization process, in terms of the issues of staffing of management team, and functional backup from the headquarters in many cases.

Staffing would always be a problem even for a global corporation in China, especially for senior management positions, though it is supposed that global corporations are always attractive to high caliber and ambitious talents everywhere. Unfortunately the local supply of this elite group of labor is far less than the demand posed by foreign investments here and as a result, imported management talent from overseas would be the definite quickest solution. At least it sounds so in the eyes of many top executives who are responsible for the China project.

To show the strategic importance of their respective China project in fulfilling their objective of going global, many multinational corporations are sending their 'top guns' who have proven track records in their specialized areas and functions and expect them to take good care their businesses in China and grow the businesses as planned. Many of these 'mercenaries' would be manifestly quite professional and experienced in business sector of the western world, adept at most advance management skills, proficient in figures of all types, and etc., however, many of them, as might have been shown in many cases, are not very good at running a business that requires them to do it in a way like virtually starting a totally new business from scratch.

These expatriate executives at the top of the China operations could have refined risk management skills, strong business acumen, and excellent knowledge of all business processes to start their own business smoothly, but they seems not practicing them in their capacities in leading the China business for the global giants in the business sector, as if they just do not feel the necessity of doing so. Overlooking the necessity of a comprehension of 'expanding business in China resembles starting a brand new business' would handicap the entire management teams in reacting to the dynamics of China market everyday.

Two major reasons can be summarized as to why such a philosophy would be needed.

Firstly, China is not a well-established market and its macro business environment keeps changing all the time. New policies and regulations are continuously exercised with a view to better 'regulating' the market by central government and local administration respectively; and some of them would be contradicting and confusing as they are. Distribution channels in various industries are being restructured and most the time these changes are just difficult for local enterprises to follow, not to mention foreign investments. A thorough understanding of this fact requires the management team to do their homework with a more critical eye prior to any decision taking, as they would do in starting up a new business. Eyes and ears are kept wide open, more comprehensive plans are worked out, executions of particular plans are better attended, various scenarios in the industry are closely assessed, and most importantly, financial figures are rigidly reviewed from time to time. It is exactly because of the uncertainties imparted in the developing market that foreign investors need to ready themselves with a set of precautions to tackle all upcoming surprises.

Secondly, a very disappointing phenomenon that exists in most foreign investing companies in China though hardly would it be admitted is that support offered by the headquarters would be rather minimal in reality, far less than the extent as supposed by the senior management sitting in the headquarters, and the local management crawling their ways ahead. No matter whether these expatriate executives were once the most respectful high-ranking executives in the headquarters before they are re-located and no matter how well they had been doing in dealing with their peers in the headquarters, it is always a saying 'out of sight, out of mind'. Their influences are diminishing in the headquarters right after they are removed from their positions there. The challenge is that it is exactly the critical moment for a new developing business in China at its infant stage to get as much support as possible so that it could be put on track at full force soonest. Ironically enough, there are numerous real stories which foreign investing companies fail to survive, many projects fall apart, product launches get cancelled, shipment are delayed, and many of them are, at least partially, attributed to that collaboration from the headquarters is not in place in time. It would be noticeable that in the eyes of many staff working in the headquarters or other affiliated companies for a multinational corporation in United States or Europe, the new organization formed thousand miles away in China is no longer be their peers and instead, they are kind of competition now. Perhaps, it has been taken so seriously that they are regarded as rivalries competing the appraisal from the senior management now, and posing threat to their job opportunities in the long run. This kind of thinking would be widely spread over the operational level seriously enough to interfere the normalcy of daily operation of a company going globally.

Before efforts would be put to successfully adjust the mindset of the majority of the working teams in the headquarters, and collaboration between headquarters and local organization in China would be established by some means, with which I have serious doubts on its possibility of success, a reliance on their individual bonds and connection with the headquarters to make things happen would entrap themselves into a very passive position to the local changes of all kinds.

Hence, it is one of the major responsibilities for the senior management of the global corporations to make sure that there are channels of constant communication and paths of assistance ready in place in-between the parties from the very beginning of their China project to co-ordinate all the activities in process.

In addition, as far as staff deployment is concerned, top managers with entrepreneurship would be considered one of the pre-requisite before they are installed in the local organization to help grow the business, since they are supposed sometimes, if not all the time, to fight alone in the frontier without a rescue team ready to troop in whenever assistance is sought.

## *Crisis mismanagement*

As mentioned above, the very nature of the processes of transformation into market-driven economic system implants various uncertainties and unpredictability in the roads ahead of most global firms investing actively in China.

There have been many examples to illustrate that it is not yet uncommon that enterprises in many industries might be caught by surprise of a sudden repeal or amendment or enforcement of business-related laws or rules or regulations in specific industries from the administration without any prior notice, and foreign investments are not immune to this hardship as well. For instance, not long ago the central government had caught one big joint venture of over-the-counter drugs in Tianjin totally by surprise, by announcing suddenly the prohibition of selling and marketing of any over-the-counter drugs that contains particular ingredient hazardous to human health. It was totally a nightmare to this joint venture company, which have been the market leader in the segment of OTC drugs on cold and flu. It required that all merchandises in the market had to be retrieved by the manufacturer immediately and it led to a disastrous consequence of that all production activities of this flagship product in the entire plant were next to a complete halt.

In general, the local management of foreign investment is lacking in a sense of crisis when they are managing their businesses in China. Though they would be working brilliantly in taking corrective measures when there comes any crisis in front of them, they are not well prepared to put effort to anticipate the possible crisis. However, preventative measures derived from a good assessment on potential risk and crisis can always enable the companies in a more active position when there is any signs of crisis coming or so.

Before the legal system of China is going to evolve into a state where their legal institution is comparable to the common standards of the western world in the coming decades, foreign investors have to equip themselves with an ability to manage potential risk and crisis. It is imperative that the local management team, as the representative of the best interest of the foreign investment and the company itself, calls for not only the capability of reacting with corrective measures to any crisis arising effectively and efficiently, but also the competence of anticipating and assessing the potential risk and crisis whenever necessary.

# Staffing is getting easier than ever

A nation populated with 1.3 billions people would mean a huge number of work force available to each industry and its attractiveness to western businessmen just multiply as far as its relatively cheap labor cost is concerned. Hundreds of universities and colleges across the territory are supplying the local job market with hundreds of thousands of college graduates in various fields of professions every year. In some industries of technology-related fields, it can be admitted that China is one of the countries where you can find many jaded local talents in hi-tech fields like nuclear technology, electronic engineering, biotech science and so forth.

Nevertheless, there are always two sides of a coin. One's professional and/or technical knowledge of his specialized areas is an asset to himself and his employer, but some basic qualities and skills, not limited to be an application in his work but his daily life, should be at least equally important to both parties as well. These qualities consist of one's attitude towards his work, his role perception in a team, his foresightedness on career development, and these skills include his interpersonal skills in his peers, leadership skills over his subordinates, and management skills in his capacity as a whole.

China as one of the most ancient countries has been bumping into troubles in the past centuries for various reasons and it had been left behind since the industrialization process took place in the west. Decades of exposure to a conventional socialistic system has stereotyped the majority of Chinese people in their ways of thinking and their behavior patterns. Old habits are hard to kill and its impact on the youths nowadays would yet be ominously overshadowing the very inner natures deeply suppressed in their brains. Many of the young generations are still tuning their minds and attitudes in a way that they could better synchronize with the western world gradually, though it has to be a very time consuming process. The nation itself is trying hard learning as well. It appears that when it is eagerly picking up with every effort to develop relentlessly in lots of areas of applied sciences for decades; they have miscalculated the significance of management science as a core substance in economic development until a decade ago. It is strange yet not common that in many local universities dated literatures and materials are still widely used in classes by business faculties. 'Management as a subject on science' might be still finding its place in the minds of the majority of Chinese people, until they are eventually experiencing its wondrous power in the new millennium.

Upgrading the quality of a people must rely on its very own hands and seems too irrelevant to concern any foreign investment for abroad. However, it would bother all foreign investments in their daily operation as long as they are hiring local people in the organization. It cannot be regarded as a matter of take-or-leave-it type. People are the most valuable asset in a company and it must be one of the greatest words of wisdom to describe life in business world.

Since most foreign investors are going to recruit local labor to carry out their business plans in China, human resources management is definitely an issue. As a matter of fact, an unwise and thoughtless policy on human resources management in China would be the ultimate cause of many problems that would be avoided otherwise.

## Good command of foreign language

Most foreign investors are quite concerned about their staff's command foreign languages, and many times they just prioritize this requirement too much to look into their other skills and abilities which would be far more essential for them to really perform their jobs adequately.

There is no doubt that it would be pleasant experiences meeting local Chinese managers who speak fluent English and expatriates are of course more than willing to work with someone who speaks the same language so they feel less mentally anxious about their inabilities to communicate articulately with their colleague, and are freed from a sense of insecurity and isolation from their local peers. Nonetheless, there are two facts that foreign investments had better bear in mind when looking for high caliber local employees to fill in key management positions: Firstly, there are yet too less talents in the job market who are fluent in foreign language and equally conversant with modern management skills than supposed, and secondly; there are a bit too many who speak English well but possess substandard management skills across the territory. There two hard facts combine to escalate the possibility of hiring falsely an incumbent whose job performance would eventually disappoint his supervisors in the company if he is unwisely appraised on his proficiency in language.

In my opinion, mastery in practical knowledge of a profession should always overweigh the proficiency in language if it comes to a dilemma for a foreign investor to pick the right candidate. After all, the latter could be trained in a shorter period of time and a mistake caused by his handicap in language would probably be much less lethal to the entire company than an insensible decision made by a substandard manager.

## Recruitment and appraisal

From the 80's up to the early years of 90's, many local Chinese had been dreaming of an opportunity of working in joint venture companies because it was crystal clear to them that foreign investments would be offering much more generous compensation scheme than any state owned enterprises would. Yet, some of them were very much bothered with their concern about job security in the future, since the general public would conceive that quitting from a state enterprise was an obtrusive action at the expense of one's lifetime employment. It was and still is a tough question for a typical Chinese and it is even tougher for a Chinese manager who have done so much to come to where he is now on the corporate ladder. Interestingly, this way of thinking freed coincidently the foreign investments from many troubles of picking the wrong incumbents at that time, even without a strict process in recruitment. It turned out that those who would consider a career in foreign investments were mostly young and ambitious and carefree young Chinese managers. They dared to harbor big hopes in career in these multinational companies and were dedicated to take whatever challenges they are faced, without any hesitancy that other might have held. These new bloods were indeed the most valuable asset to the foreign investors now and then.

However, things that would likely go wrong are going wrong eventually. When foreign investments keeps rushing in China market, the picture has changed dramatically. Demand in high caliber talents surges at a rate that the supply of the same in the local job market would not match. Ironically enough, many foreign investments have a subconscious inclination to setting up organization proportional to the total population size of the nation regardless of their business size; some would succumb to the harsh requirement imposed by authorities on take-over of local staff; and etc. etc. Gate-keeping function on recruitment is loosened somehow and the overall quality of staff is deteriorating as the organization keeps expanding.

At present, it would be said that foreign investments are losing its appeal to the job market as they were once the only few in China who can afford to pay generously to their employee, when more and more state enterprises are adopting motivation tools of the western world. On the other hand, they are now more likely perceived to be just a new branch of employers who are serving with a lifetime-like employment as the state enterprises were in the past, while there you find more and more average, if not incapable or substandard, staffs kept and promoted everywhere.

A big organization on management level usually triggers a problem of low efficiency and it should be justified by good reasons only. It would be like a shot in one's own foot that a foreign investment fools itself by first expanding the organization beyond its optimal size and then downsizing it again so that they can claim an organization of the 'best team'.

In the meantime, a rush in localization process of your organization in China would handicap the overall performance of the organization if quality of the people on average were sacrificed.

As said before, human resources management seems a function to which less attention is paid by the top management in China. It was in general the first function area that was first localized when the idea of localization was getting popular in China few years ago. This function might not be directly related to the profit and loss statement, it is in reality your second-in-command to manage and control the most precious asset of the whole company: People. It is a saddening fact that human resources function in China is downgraded to a personnel function that is translated into a specialized division of administration on personnel matters instead. This interpretation would have been very typical for a local Chinese but it is just stunning to find out that many foreign investments would have been making the same mistake in a country where such mistake would cost them a lot to reverse. As a result, casualness in recruitment procedures and policies just expose the company to the risk of incapable staff and managers 'choking' the entire organization and dampening the business development consequently.

There have been many successful global corporations who are exercising excellent human resources policies and procedures in their western boundaries to develop continuously better organization. A rigid appraisal policy of forward thinking forms a crucial part of this strategy. However, it would simply fall apart when they are introduced in China. The reason would be a lack of solemn determination in the practice of such policies and the top management is blinded without knowing any potential risk on its most precious asset. Such situation would be as deadly as that a financial controller is kept away from any information of how the cash flow is doing in his company each month.

From my point of view, human resources strategy of the foreign investments would be as deadly essential as an operating system in a computer. No matter how powerful software programs and applications you have installed in this computer of the best hardware configuration than ever, they are next to useless if the operating system is bust by bugs. If necessary, bugs must be fixed or removed as soon as possible, before the system could be revitalized to function normally.

## Efficiency versus large organization

'Efficiency' as one of the key elements in modern capitalism is totally a new concept to China and its people. They were accustomed to the plan economy and did not bother to look over their shoulders until 20 years ago when they realized that their socialistic economic development had been so vulnerable and primitive in comparison with that of the capitalistic countries in the west. That was when they opted for opening up to the world and began to replicate the western experiences for their very survival in the international community.

Chairman Mao was strictly an advocate for the notion of 'more people can get things better done' and the country did once suffer from this paradox by turning itself into a giant machine of inefficiency to go nowhere for a long time.

While the Chinese are working hard to reverse some of their mistakes in economic development by absorbing some fundamentals in capitalism into its system, some foreign investments would surprisingly repeat its mistakes here in China. Maybe they are enticed by the deception of low labor cost and an illusion of building an empire here in China to impress their peers, so that they just do not raise an eyebrow when their organizations keep ballooning ineptly, not until they are alerted with signs of low efficiency in their businesses in China, they knit their eyebrows at the extremely high overhead costs in the report.

As known well, every organization would need to consume heavily lots of corporate resources inside the company before these resources are invested into value adding in the business processes by which customer satisfaction is maximized ultimately. A waste on a bulky organization would only lower the productivity of the entire organization and weaken your competitiveness in the market.

Some foreign investments might have realized the low efficiency in their operations in China but fail to sort out a solution to address the problem properly. Among them, some of these companies would add headcount in particular functional areas in order to keep the wheel rolling. Obviously it is just a trick to blur their own vision as playing ostrich.

Frankly speaking, if downsizing would get so popular as one of the management tool to cater for lowering efficiency in operation in many saturated western markets, it could first be applied in the emerging market like China as well.

## Executive development program

China might be in a shortage of local talents who would be ready to instantly take up more responsibilities in the foreign investments, however, there are many young Chinese managers who definitely possess the potentials for further self development. Their potentials are subject to the willingness of each foreign investor to explore.

A forward thinking in human resources management is needed when you are to organize your expatriate managers with the local team in terms of on the job coaching. Transfer of best experiences and know-how can best be done if both parties are integrated smoothly.

In addition, long-term strategy on training scheme for Chinese staff with potentials such as executive development program could be vital to raise your own strong team of local managers and take full care of your business when you and they are both ready.

It is constantly a good move to build a link with local educational institutions, as some multinational corporations have been active in doing so, so as to make the best use of this connection as a source to recruit talented Chinese for your team of the future.

0-595-26261-9